365 Games & Puzzles to Keep Your Mind Sharp

365 Games & Puzzles to Keep Your Mind Sharp

By Kim Chamberlain

kim@kimchamberlain.com
www.kimchamberlain.com

Skyhorse Publishing

Visit our website at www.skyhorsepublishing.com.

10 9 8 7 6 5 4 3

Library of Congress Cataloging-in-Publication Data is available on file.

Cover design by Rain Saukas

Print ISBN: 978-1-63450-355-6
Ebook ISBN: 978-1-63450-956-5

Printed in the United States of America

Contents

Introduction

Hello and welcome to the second in the series of the Five Minute Brain Workout, a brain training book based on word games and puzzles.

Taking care of your brain can be equally as useful as taking care of your body. By simply using five minutes at a time to stimulate and challenge your brain on a regular basis, it can help keep your mind sharp and flexible.

Doing short, varied mental activities and challenging your brain with new tasks can help improve your memory, concentration, problem-solving skills, processing speed, creativity, logic and reasoning.

To this end I have included many new and interesting puzzles to help keep your brain active and stimulated, along with some of the same types of puzzles from the first book *(The 5 Minute Brain Work-out)*, to provide a feeling of familiarity.

We learn more if three factors are present: if we are doing some-thing we enjoy; if there is repetition; if there is variety. For these reasons the book uses a games and puzzles theme aimed at people who enjoy words and language; there are ten examples of the same kind of game or puzzle; and there is a wide variety of types.

By doing both games and puzzles it will give you the discipline that comes with finding the 'correct' answer required for puzzles, along with the creativity of a range of acceptable answers that a game provides.

You have enough for twelve months' worth of working your brain, so let's get started . . .

How the book is laid out

Games & Puzzles

There are 365 exercises—enough for one a day—comprising 37 different types of word games and puzzles, spaced evenly throughout the book. 36 types have ten exercises, while the 37th has five exercises.

Levels

There are ten levels, generally increasing in difficulty as you go through the book. This means that the tenth exercise will usually be harder than the ones preceding it.

The difference between a game and a puzzle

Generally speaking a puzzle has a specific answer, like a Word Sudoku, whereas a game doesn't, and may have a number of suitable answers. For example "Find as many words as you can in a minute that rhyme with the word 'light.'" Approximately two thirds of the exercises are puzzles, while the rest are games.

Variety

There is a wide variety of types of exercises (37 to be exact) specifically devised to make your brain work in different ways and keep it alert.

Bonus

Try the three bonus puzzles at the end. They are a taster from the next book!

Answers

You will find the answers at the back of the book. The puzzles have specific answers, while the games have examples of acceptable answers.

How to use this book

First of all, feel free to use the book in any way you like, there is no right or wrong way to use it.

A suggested way is to start at the beginning and work through all the Level 1 games and puzzles, doing one a day through the levels until you reach Level 10. Or you may like to choose one type of game or puzzle and work through all ten levels, before going back to a new puzzle and doing the same.

As many of the exercises will be new to you, it's a good idea to take time to read the instructions so that you can use the 5 minutes well.

The games and puzzles will probably take you different amounts of time. Some may not take the full 5 minutes, while some are more involved and may take you slightly longer.

While the puzzles have specific answers, the games don't, which means you can continue developing your creativity by doing them more than once and getting different answers.

If you are not sure how to tackle a game or puzzle, look at the answer and work out how it is done, then you'll know how to do the next one.

As well as a way to exercise your brain, the games and puzzles can be used to challenge yourself, or simply to have fun, or you can bring in a competitive element by using a timer or doing them with others.

The exercises can be used in many settings, for example at home; in work; in social settings; in educational settings such as schools; as icebreakers and energizers in training sessions, and in therapy settings.

Level 1

ROWS AND COLUMNS 1

Fill in the column with a word that makes the rows into complete words. There are no proper nouns used. There may be more than one answer.

R	I		T
S	H		P
P	O		R
C	A		T

CONCENTRATION 1

SEQUENCE 1 Which of these sequences is the same as:

M K N L R N D N N L R B M H C

1. M K N L R D N N N L R B M H C
2. M K N L R N N D N L R B M H C
3. M K N L R N D N L N R B M H C
4. M K N L R N D N N L R B M H C
5. M K N L N R D N N L R B M H C
6. M K N L R R D N N L R B M H C

SEQUENCE 2 Which of these sequences is the same as:

N D R J S L B N V N J T S L C

1. N D R J S L B N V N N T S L C
2. N D R J S L B N V N J S T L C
3. N D R J S L B N N V J T S L C
4. N D R J S L B V V N J T S L C
5. N D R J S L B N V N J T S L C
6. N D R S J L B N V N J T S L C

VOWEL WORDS 1

Choose words that fit the categories and include the given vowel.

The vowel can be used as often as you like in the word, but it must be the only vowel used.

Vowel: **A**	
Two boys' names	
Two girls' names	
Two place names	
Two creatures' names	
Two types of food	
Two items of clothing	
A hobby or pastime	

CONTINUOUS WORDS 1

This is a list of words that have been joined together. Put the spaces in the appropriate places to work out the list of words.

FLEEFLESHISLESELLSHELFFISHLEASHSHALELASHFLASH
SELFISHSHELLHASSLESEALSHALLHALFELFAISLEFILLFLAIL
FALSESAFEFAILFALSIFYSHYYESSALESALSAFALLFLYHEAL
LEASELEAFSAILYELL

WORD IN WORD 1

Put the 3-letter words on the left hand side into the correct spaces to make 8-letter words.

<table>
<tr><td rowspan="5">OUR
EVE
HOW
OWE
ACE</td><td>F</td><td></td><td></td><td></td><td>L</td><td>E</td><td>S</td><td>S</td></tr>
<tr><td>J</td><td></td><td></td><td></td><td>N</td><td>A</td><td>L</td><td>S</td></tr>
<tr><td>C</td><td></td><td></td><td></td><td>R</td><td>I</td><td>N</td><td>G</td></tr>
<tr><td>R</td><td></td><td></td><td></td><td>R</td><td>E</td><td>N</td><td>D</td></tr>
<tr><td>S</td><td></td><td></td><td></td><td>E</td><td>R</td><td>E</td><td>D</td></tr>
</table>

WORD RHYME 1

Find as many words as you can that rhyme with the given word. Use a timer, and take a minute for each of the five words. Note that different words rhyme in different accents, so choose words that rhyme in your accent. Decide if you want to include proper nouns or not. You can include rhyming words with different spellings, for example REED and READ.

NOSE	
LIGHT	
NOTE	
SENT	
ICE	

HALF WORDS 1

Join two half words together to form five lots of 6-letter words.

A E R	S E N
A G E	B E H
I A L	B E R
A V E	A R I
B A R	E N G

1. ______________________________

2. ______________________________

3. ______________________________

4. ______________________________

5. ______________________________

Level 1

X WORDS 1

Place the correct words in the rows in the grid so that both diagonals spell a four-letter word reading from top to bottom.

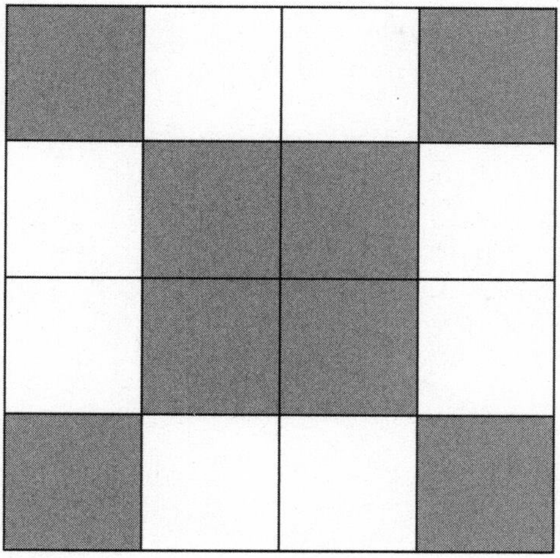

TEXT

MEAT

MAST

TRUE

ALPHABET TEASERS 1

D

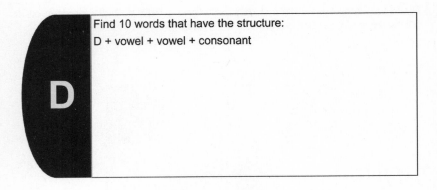

Find 10 words that have the structure:

D + vowel + vowel + consonant

J

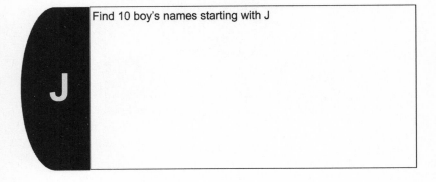

Find 10 boy's names starting with J

Level 1

ANAGRAM GRID 1

Solve the anagrams and place them into the correct spaces in the grid. One letter has been placed for you.

ROWNS

ROWBN

ROWAR

ROYRW

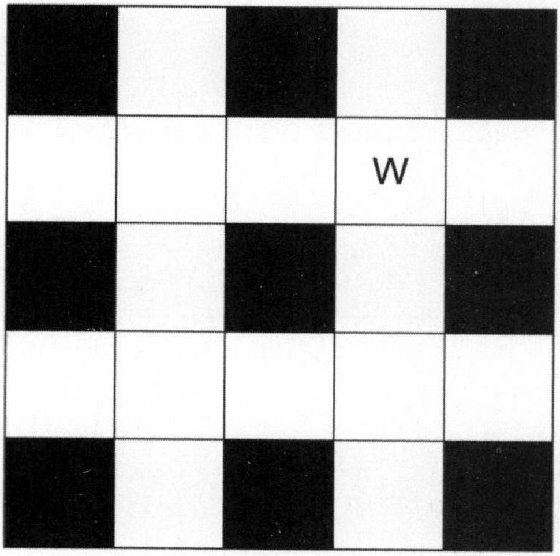

I LIKE ... 1

All the items *'I like'* have a connection that the items *'I don't like'* do not have. Can you work out the connection?

I LIKE ...	... BUT I DON'T LIKE
coffee	tea
boots	shoes
yellow	red
addition	subtraction
college	university
rabbits	hares
carrots	peas
mutton	lamb

WORD FLOW 1

Think of five 5-letter words that start with the letters on the left and end with the letter in the middle. Then think of five 5-letter words that start with the letter in the middle and end with the letters on the right. Avoid using proper nouns.

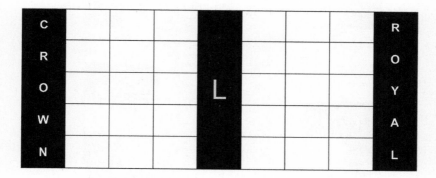

C								R
R								O
O				L				Y
W								A
N								L

RHYME TIME 1

Each row in the grid contains two words that rhyme—an adjective and a noun.

Solve the clues then slot the words into the grid so that the gray column also contains two rhyming words. The first one has been done for you.

1		B	I	G	F	I	G	
2								
3								
4								
5								
6								
7								

CLUES

1 LARGE FRUIT 3,3

2 OVERCAST SONGBIRD 4,4

3 UNCOOKED FACIAL BONE 3,3

4 VERY WARM DISH 3,3

5 HIGHEST FLOOR CLEANER 3,3

6 ANGRY PARENT 3,3

7 BASE DIGIT 3,3

MEMORY CIRCLE 1

Study the grid and remember the shapes, the words and where they are positioned. Then turn the page and answer the questions.

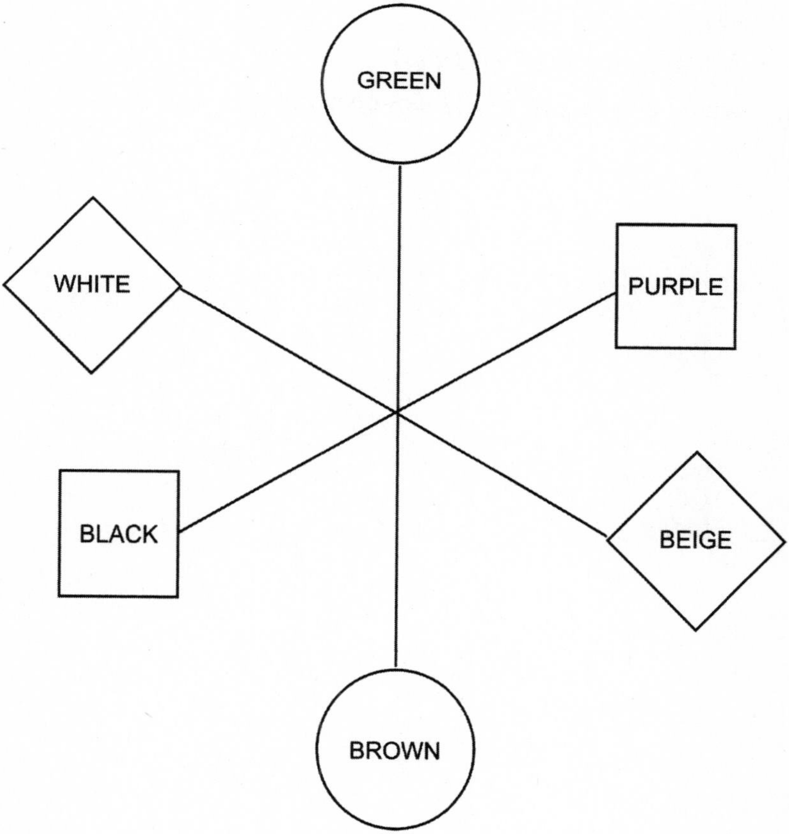

MEMORY CIRCLE 1

Questions

1. What shape is opposite BEIGE?
2. Which two words are in the squares?
3. Going in a clockwise direction, which word is 2 spaces after BLACK?
4. Which shape is BROWN in?
5. Which word comes between GREEN and BEIGE?

WORD CREATION 1

Taking the **last 2** letters of a word, use them as the **first 2** letters of a new word of any length. For example the word after HEALTH may be THREE. Don't repeat words and avoid using proper nouns.

Within 5 minutes can you create at least 50 words?

ARNICA				
				50 words!

VOLVOGRAMS 1

Volvograms are words that spell another word when read backwards, for example BIN and NIB. Work out each pair of volvograms from the clues given, and then slot them into the crossword grid.

Angry barrier (3) (3)

Eager female singer (4) (4)

Evil spirit existed (5) (5)

TRIANGLES 1

Each triangle contains a 3-letter, 4-letter and 5-letter word, placed in the direction of the arrows. Put the words into the correct triangles.

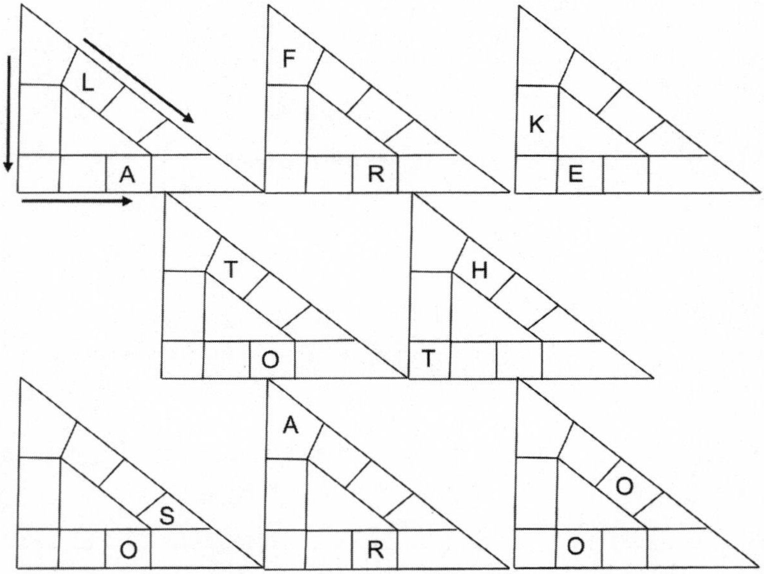

3-letter words	4-letter words	5-letter words
ANT	AMOK	ALARM
ASP	NOOK	ALERT
CAP	PART	CHARM
CAT	PROP	CLASP
FAN	TRAM	FIRST
FLY	TRIM	FLOCK
SEA	YELP	SHARP
SKY	YURT	STOCK

NINE WORDS 1

Write one or more complete sentences with words containing 1 through to 9 letters.

No. of letters	Sentence
1	
2	
3	
4	
5	
6	
7	
8	
9	

MARRIED WITH CHILDREN 1

Take 2 letters from each parent's name and combine them to form a 4-letter name of their child. The (m) or (f) indicates the gender. There may be more than one answer.

For example PAUL & RHEA = LARA

EVAN & TESS (m)

RORY & DINA (f)

ANDY & MARY (m)

DREW & GINA (f)

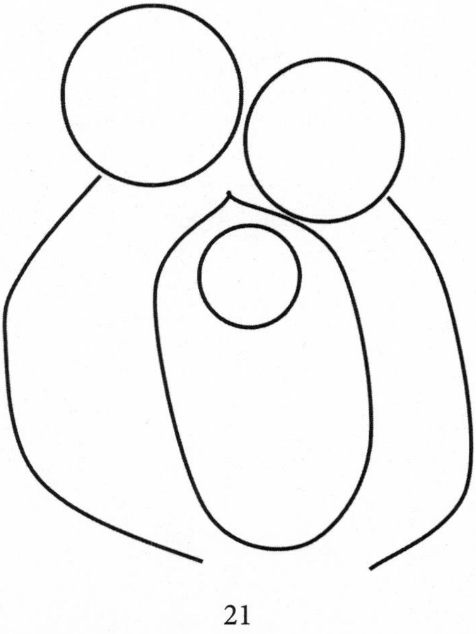

LETTER CHANGE 1

Change one letter in each of the four words so that they belong to a group of similar words. The letter to change has been underlined. The first one has been done for you.

HONEY	RENT	CORN	DOTE
MONEY	*CENT*	*COIN*	*NOTE*

VEST	LUGE	GREET	BIN

LOOK	HOVEL	STORE	TAKE

HOOK	BIKE	FOIL	PEACH

TOAD	PATE	LAKE	ROUSE

DIAMOND WORDS 1

Find 9 words that fit the diamond grid. Avoid using the same word more than once, and words that are proper nouns.

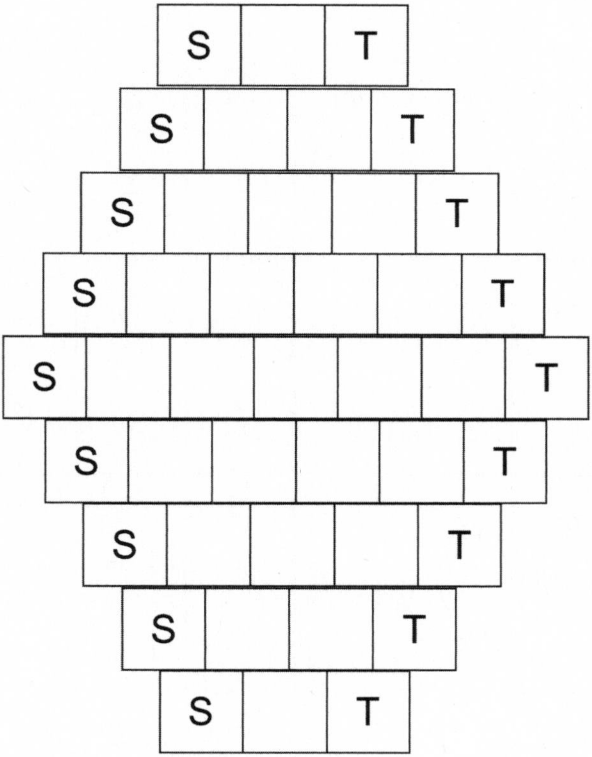

MINI WORD SUDOKU 1

Place the letters from the 6-letter word ANSWER in the grid so that each column, each row, and each of the six 2×3 sub-grids contains all of the 6 letters from the word.

		W		S	
N				E	W
S					
					E
R	S				N
	E		A		

LETTER SHUFFLE 1

A saying has been placed in the grid in a continuous string, going from left to right, and reading from top to bottom. The 5 letters in the shaded squares have been rearranged.

The word lengths are: 2, 3, 7, 10, 3, 5

D	I	N	O	T
O	E	L	I	E
V	E	E	V	E
R	Y	T	H	O
N	G	Y	I	U
T	H	B	N	K

Saying:

____

____

____

LETTER BOXES 1

Take one letter from each box to form a 4-letter word. Topic: Boys' names
The first one has been done for you.

M T D G	O I A A	V R K N	Y E E Y
D	A	V	E

SPEED WORDS 1

Choose 10 words that fit the criteria given. Choose words that are not proper nouns. Use a different word for each question.

Choose a word that:		
1	Begins with 'HE' and has 2 syllables	
2	Includes a double 'S'	
3	Ends in 'OPER'	
4	Begins with T and has 6 letters	
5	Ends in 'LY'	
6	Includes the letters 'OIC'	
7	Has 5 letters with 'X' in the middle	
8	Rhymes with 'MANNER'	
9	Is an anagram of 'VELON'	
10	Has one syllable and begins and ends with 'K'	

CLUES 1

Solve the clues then find the letters, which are placed randomly in the grid. Cross them off, circle them, or color in the square as you find them. The first one has been done for you.

CLUES

1. Male relative = UNCLE
2. Zodiac sign
3. Big cat
4. Month

R	R	R	(N)	A
S	(U)	Y	L	(L)
P	I	E	(C)	E
O	U	(E)	A	F
B	R	E	A	D

WORD PLUS WORD 1

Add a 3-letter word to the initial letter so that it also makes a 4-letter word, for example A + HEM. Make each of the 3-letter words different. Avoid using plurals and proper nouns.

A			
B			
C			
D			
E			
F			
G			
H			
I			
J			

MISSING ALPHABET 1

There are 9 words, each having a different letter of the alphabet missing. Work out which letter goes in each word. None of the words are proper nouns.

The letters are provided so you can cross off each one as you find it.

W I N _	S _ N K	C _ N E
C A L _	_ O A T	_ E A L
S _ O P	P A _ K	_ A I N

A B C D E F G H I

SQUIDS 1

Here we have a square grid (squid). Can you place the letters in the correct squares so that the grid makes 4 words that read both horizontally and vertically?

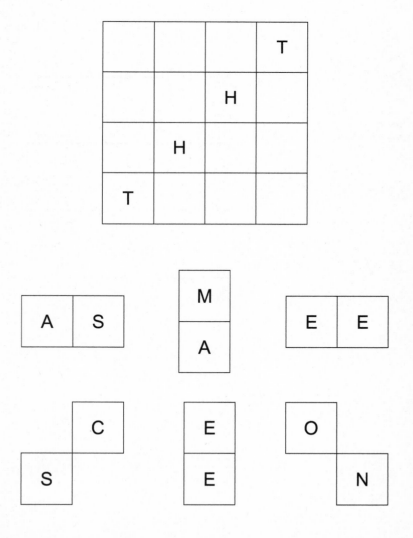

			T
		H	
	H		
T			

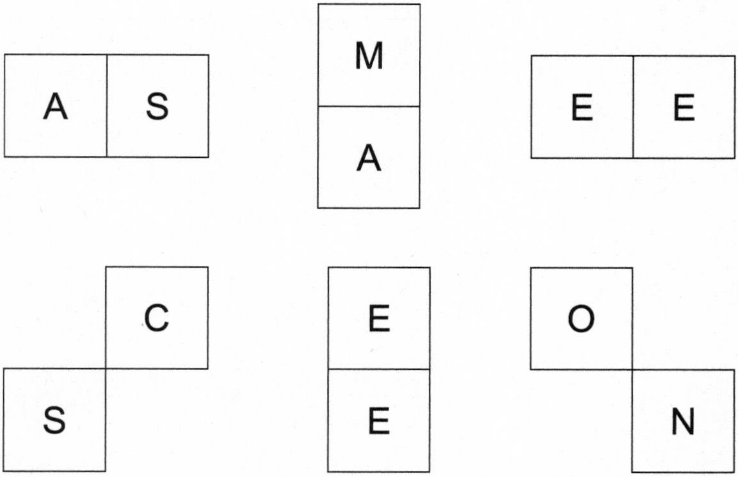

SENTENCE MAKER 1

Make up a sentence with words that fit into the structures given, where C stands for Consonant, and V stands for Vowel.

For example the sentence SHE LIKES CATS would fit into the structure CCV CVCVC CVCC. Proper nouns are allowed, and you can put punctuation anywhere in the sentence if you would like to.

C C ______________________________

C V C V ______________________________

V C ______________________________

C V C V C ______________________________

WORKING IT OUT 1

Work out what these phrases have in common.

Mark went in Jon’s hut.

All the kids got up.

“What he did to us,”

Sally wept “is so hurtful;

Can’t settle, it’s no fun.”

SYLLABLE WORDS 1

The words to find each have 3 syllables. The last syllable or section of one word forms the first syllable or section of the next, for example WONDERFUL and FULFILLING.

Starting in the centre, draw a continuous line from one word to the next. There are four words to find. The first one has been done for you.

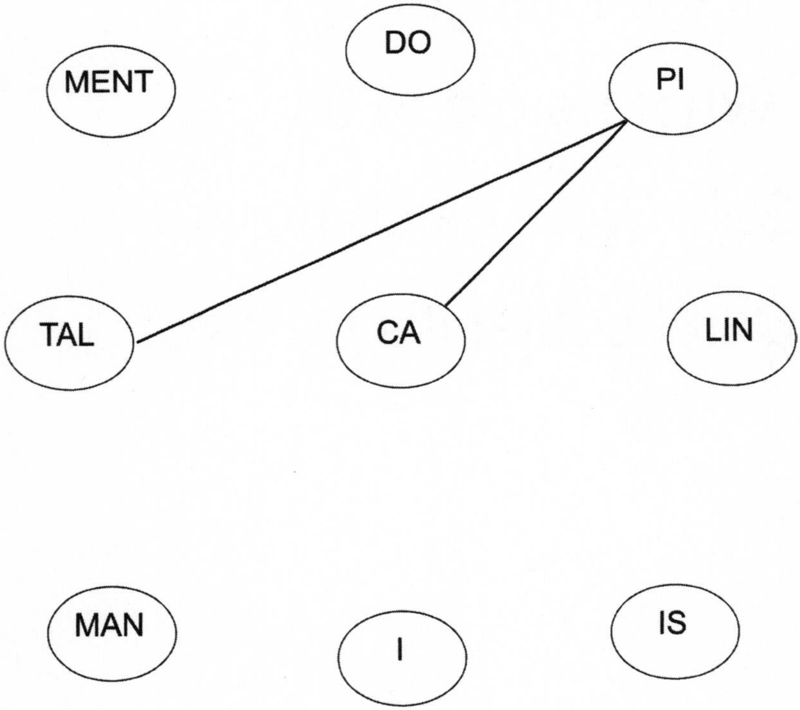

POETRY 1

Make up a poem with two stanzas of four lines each, where the second and fourth lines in each stanza rhyme. Example:

I tried to find a jeep

But could only find a car

It wasn't very good

And didn't get me far.

The first line is given:

My mother likes to bake

MISSING LETTERS 1

Two letters are missing from the first set of words, and a different two letters are missing from the second set of words. What are the letters?

SET 1

__ A T H E __

__ I N G E __

__ A R M E __

__ R I A __

SET 2

__ R I A __

__ I N G __ E

__ I T __ E

__ A __ E

WORD TRAIL 1

Find the 6 words listed in the grid starting with the circled letter. The last letter of one word forms the first letter of the next word.

Words go horizontally backward or forwards, or vertically upwards or downwards.

(T)	R	E	R	U
E	E	A	T	S
T	W	C	A	T
S	T	I	T	A
I	W	T	N	U

TREAT

TRUST

TACIT

TAUNT

TWIST

TWEET

THREE LETTERS 1

How many words can you think of that contain the three given letters in this order? They do not need to be together in the word, can occur anywhere, but need to be in this order. For example if the letters were ITE, the words could be ITEm; bITE, InnovaTE, sIsTEr, and so on.

Aim to avoid proper nouns.

You have two options here. You can spend one minute on each set of three letters, or you can choose one set of letters and spend five minutes on it.

A R T	
S I N	
A I G	
L A T	
T O E	

LETTER SWAP 1

Three letters in each phrase have been swapped. Can you work out which three you can swap back to make another sentence. For example in the sentence CORY WOULD TALK, the letters C, W and T can be swapped to form TORY COULD WALK.

MIX BEN WITH A SOY

IT'S FUNNY IN TRANCE, SAMMY

Level 2

ROWS AND COLUMNS 2

Fill in the column with a word that makes the rows into complete words. There are no proper nouns used. There may be more than one answer.

S		U	N
P		U	R
A		E	D
M		N	E
S		U	B

CONCENTRATION 2

SEQUENCE 1 Which of these sequences is the same as:

mAnAEDUoNArdDAR

1. mAnAEDUONArddAR

2. mANAEDUoNArdDAR

3. mAnAeDUoNArDDAR

4. mAnAEDUoANrdDAR

5. mAnAEDUoNArdDAR

6. mAnaEDUoNArdDAR

SEQUENCE 2 Which of these sequence is the same as:

DoRNaOonNEemErE

1. DoRNaOOnNEemErE

2. DoRNaOoNNEemErE

3. DoRNaOonNEemErE

4. DoRNaOonNEemrEE

5. DoRnaOonNEemErE

6. DoRNaOonNeEmErE

CONTINUOUS WORDS 2

Choose words that fit the categories and include the given vowel.

The vowel can be used as often as you like in the word, but it must be the only vowel used.

Vowel: **E**	
Two boys' names	
Two girls' names	
Two place names	
Two creatures' names	
Two types of food	
Two items of clothing	
A hobby or pastime	

CONTINUOUS WORDS 2

This is a list of words that have been joined together. Put the spaces in the appropriate places to work out the list of words.

LATHEAREAHEALTHTHEYTALLLETTERTREETRYRE-
ALTYTHERETHREELEATHERTELLHEATHEARTALTER
RATTLERAYTARTALLYHEARTHRATHERTALLYYELLYE
AREARLYLYREALERTETHERHALLLATERRATETEART
EETHTRAY

WORD IN WORD 2

Put the 4-letter words on the left hand side into the correct spaces to make 8-letter words.

<table>
<tr><td rowspan="6">SHIN
POLO
ROOT
SENT
PLOD
REAM</td><td>A</td><td>B</td><td></td><td></td><td></td><td></td><td>E</td><td>E</td></tr>
<tr><td>S</td><td>C</td><td></td><td></td><td></td><td></td><td>E</td><td>D</td></tr>
<tr><td>T</td><td>O</td><td></td><td></td><td></td><td></td><td>G</td><td>Y</td></tr>
<tr><td>I</td><td>M</td><td></td><td></td><td></td><td></td><td>E</td><td>S</td></tr>
<tr><td>U</td><td>P</td><td></td><td></td><td></td><td></td><td>E</td><td>D</td></tr>
<tr><td>L</td><td>A</td><td></td><td></td><td></td><td></td><td>G</td><td>S</td></tr>
</table>

WORD RHYME 2

Find as many words as you can that rhyme with the given word. Use a timer, and take a minute for each of the five words. Note that different words rhyme in different accents, so choose words that rhyme in your accent. Decide if you want to include proper nouns or not. You can include rhyming words with different spellings, for example REED and READ.

WAIT	
MINE	
CONE	
EAT	
FIVE	

Level 2

HALF WORDS 2

Join two half words together to form six lots of 6-letter words.

L	O	W		L	A	Y
A	E	R		A	I	R
A	L	E		L	I	N
E	R	S		I	M	P
W	A	Y		A	T	E
E	A	R		W	A	L

1. ______________________________
2. ______________________________
3. ______________________________
4. ______________________________
5. ______________________________
6. ______________________________

X WORDS 2

Place the correct words in the rows in the grid so that both diagonals spell a four-letter word reading from top to bottom.

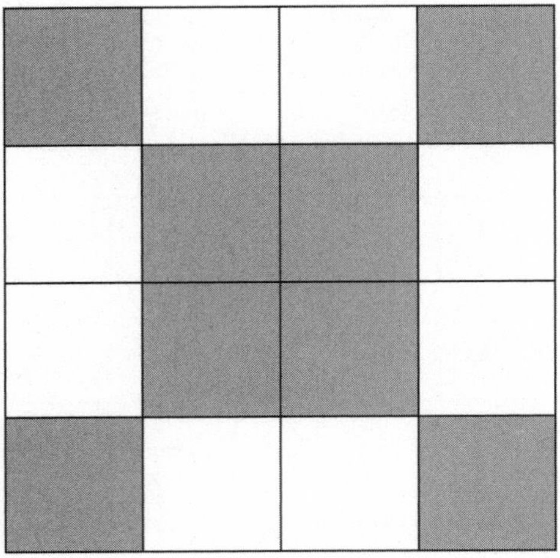

DUET

JAIL

PROP

DAME

ALPHABET TEASERS 2

B

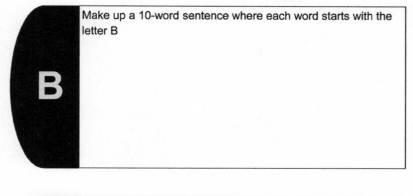

Make up a 10-word sentence where each word starts with the letter B

F

Find 10 words that end with FF

ANAGRAM GRID 2

Solve the anagrams and place them into the correct spaces in the grid.
One letter has been placed for you.

HEROT

HHATE

TORTE

ETEHT

LIKE ... 2

All the items '*I like*' have a connection that the items *'I don't like'* do not have. Can you work out the connection?

I LIKE ...	... BUT I DON'T LIKE
fantastic	great
strawberry	grape
elegant	chic
magazine	book
Oregon	Maine
basketball	squash
apartment	house
burgundy	brown

WORD FLOW 2

Think of five 5-letter words that start with the letters on the left and end with the letter in the middle. Then think of five 5-letter words that start with the letter in the middle and end with the letters on the right. Avoid using proper nouns.

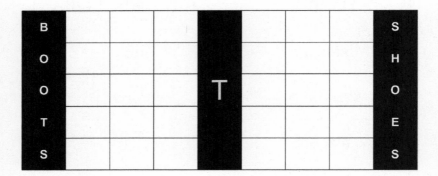

B								S
O								H
O				T				O
T								E
S								S

RHYME TIME 2

Each row in the grid contains two words that rhyme—an adjective and a noun.

Solve the clues then slot the words into the grid so that the gray column also contains two rhyming words.

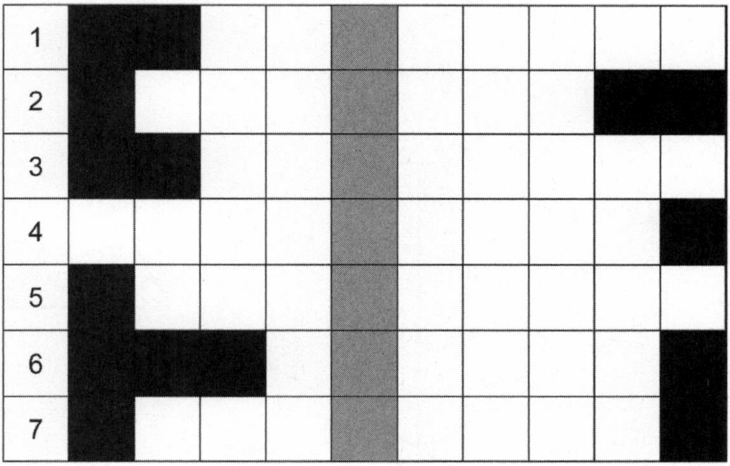

CLUES

1 PALE RED FURRY ANIMAL 4,4

2 REAL WATER DROPS 4,3

3 LOWER CITY 4,4

4 INCORRECT TUNE 5,4

5 TOTAL DIGGER 5,4

6 DROLL STAR 3,3

7 GREEN COIN 4,4

MEMORY CIRCLE 2

Study the grid and remember the shapes, the words and where they are positioned. Then turn the page and answer the questions.

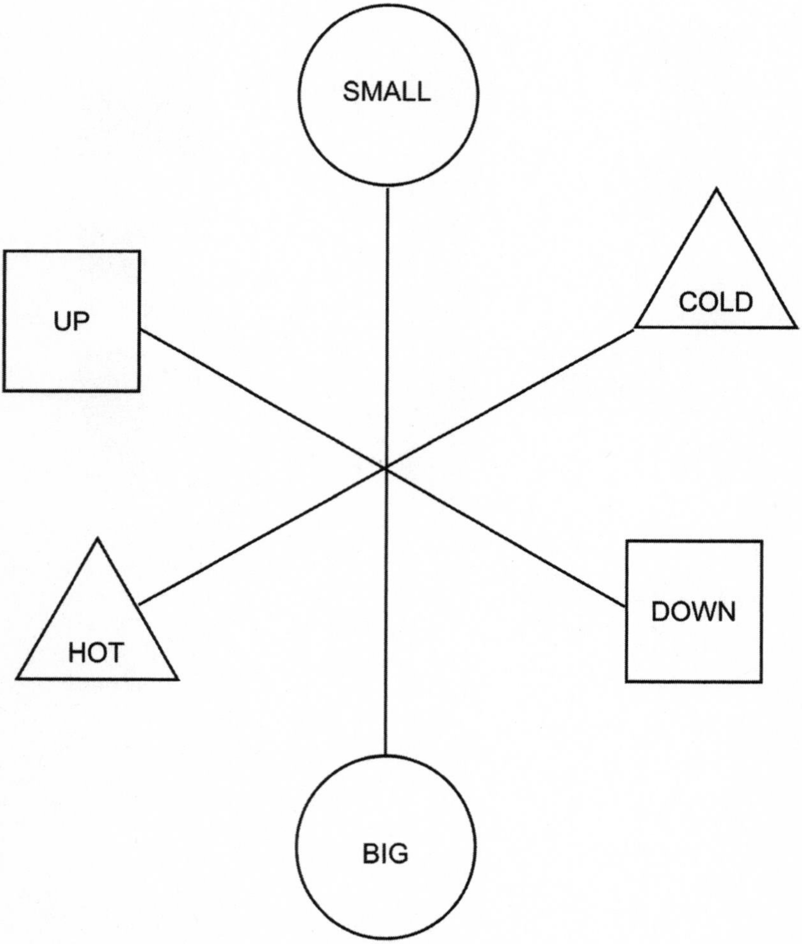

MEMORY CIRCLE 2

Questions

1. What shape is the word UP in?
2. Which two words are in the triangles?
3. Going in a clockwise direction, which word comes after DOWN?
4. Which word is between UP and COLD?
5. Going in a clockwise direction, which word comes after BIG?

WORD CREATION 2

Taking the 2nd and 3rd letters of a word, use them as the first 2 letters of a new word of any length. For example the word after HEALTH may be EARLY. Don't repeat words and avoid using proper nouns.

Within 5 minutes can you create at least 40 words?

CARD				
				40 words!

Level 2

VOLVOGRAMS 2

Volvograms are words that spell another word when read backwards, for example BIN and NIB. Work out each pair of volvograms from the clues given, and then slot them into the crossword grid.

Lotion for limb (3) (3)		
Hence, a monster (4) (4)		
Royal alcohol (5) (5)		

TRIANGLES 2

Each triangle contains a 3-letter, 4-letter and 5-letter word, placed in the direction of the arrows. Put the words into the correct triangles.

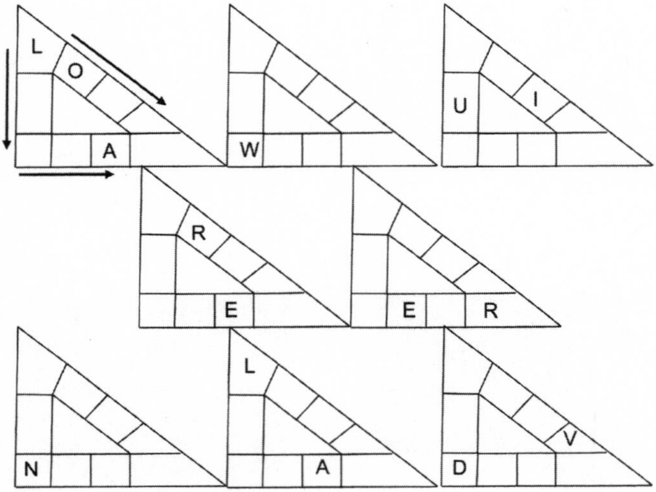

3-letter words	4-letter words	5-letter words
COT	DEED	COVER
COW	DONE	CREST
DEN	NEED	DRIVE
DID	NICE	DRUID
LOT	TEAR	LEAST
LOW	TEAT	LOVER
SUD	WEAR	SHIED
SUN	WEST	SHINE

Level 2

NINE WORDS 2

Write one or more complete sentences with words of any length, starting with the letters given.

Letters	Sentence
A	
B	
C	
D	
E	
F	
G	
H	
I	

MARRIED WITH CHILDREN 2

Take 2 letters from each parent's name and combine them to form a 4-letter name of their child. The (m) or (f) indicates the gender. There may be more than one answer.

OTTO & RUBY (m)	
ALEC & SUZY (f)	
HUGO & LENA (m)	
BART & HOPE (f)	

LETTER CHANGE 2

Change one letter in each of the four words so that they belong to a group of similar words. The letter to change has been underlined.

SILK	WAFER	TEN	TOFFEE

FORTH	LAST	MOUTH	NEST

MOAT	HAM	GROVE	SCARE

HEN	WOKEN	BOSS	GILLS

GLUE	RID	PINE	WHINE

DIAMOND WORDS 2

Find 11 words that fit the diamond grid. Avoid using the same word more than once, and words that are proper nouns.

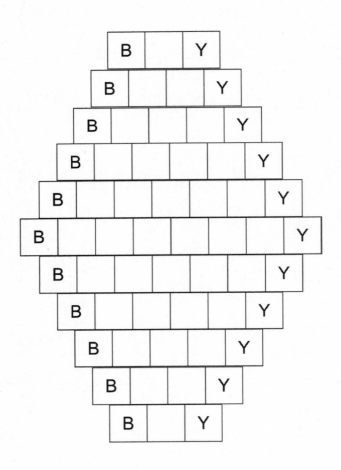

B		Y					
B			Y				
B				Y			
B					Y		
B						Y	
B							Y
B						Y	
B					Y		
B				Y			
B			Y				
B		Y					

Level 2

MINI WORD SUDOKU 2

Place the letters from the 6-letter word **DESIGN** in the grid so that each column, each row, and each of the six 2×3 sub-grids contains all of the 6 letters from the word.

		D			G
		S			
S	N		G		
		I		N	E
			N		
D			I		

LETTER SHUFFLE 2

A saying has been placed in the grid in a continuous string, going from left to right, and reading from top to bottom. The 5 letters in the shaded squares have been rearranged.

The word lengths are: 9, 2, 7, 2, 10

S	I	M	E	T
O	M	E	S	W
E	S	U	R	V
I	V	E	B	G
F	O	R	I	E
T	T	Y	N	G

Saying:

____

____

____

SPEED WORDS 2

Choose 10 words that fit the criteria given. Choose words that are not proper nouns. Use a different word for each question.

Choose a word that:		
1	Begins with 'TY' and has 2 syllables	
2	Ends with 'TY' and has 2 syllables	
3	Has the structure: vowel 'X' vowel consonant consonant	
4	Contains 3 'P's	
5	Has 2 syllables and ends with 'H'	
6	Starts with 'N' and reads the same forward and backward	
7	Fits into C ______P _ E	
8	Is 4 letters long and doesn't have a vowel	
9	Is an anagram of 'OURHAT'	
10	Has two syllables and begins and ends with 'K'	

LETTER BOXES 2

Take one letter from each box to form a 4-letter word. Topic: Girls' names

T R B M	A I E O	S R N T	E A Y H

CLUES 2

Solve the clues then find the letters, which are placed randomly in the grid. Cross them off, circle them, or color in the square as you find them.

CLUES

1. Deadly sin
2. Fruit
3. Shape
4. Educational establishment

G	G	G	O	P
E	I	E	O	E
C	L	E	A	N
D	L	X	A	R
H	E	R	O	N

WORD PLUS WORD 2

Add a 3-letter word to the initial letter so that it also makes a 4-letter word, for example A + HEM. Make each of the 3-letter words different. Avoid using plurals and proper nouns.

K			
L			
M			
N			
O			
P			
R			
S			
T			
U			

MISSING ALPHABET 2

There are 9 words, each having a different letter of the alphabet missing. Work out which letter goes in each word. None of the words are proper nouns.

The letters are provided so you can cross off each one as you find it.

_OSE	BO_T	_ELY
_OKE	HO_E	_UIT
IFE	STO_	RAC_

J K L M N O P Q R

SQUIDS 2

Can you place the letters in the correct squares so that the grid makes 4 words that read both horizontally and vertically?

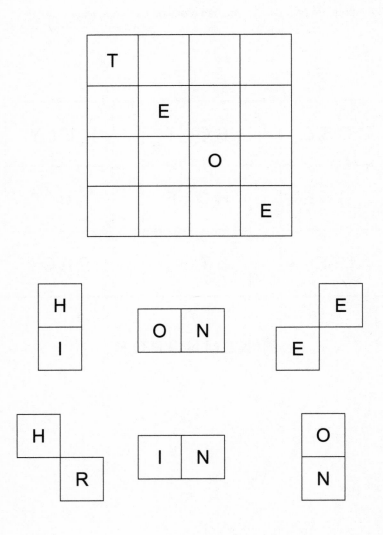

T			
	E		
		O	
			E

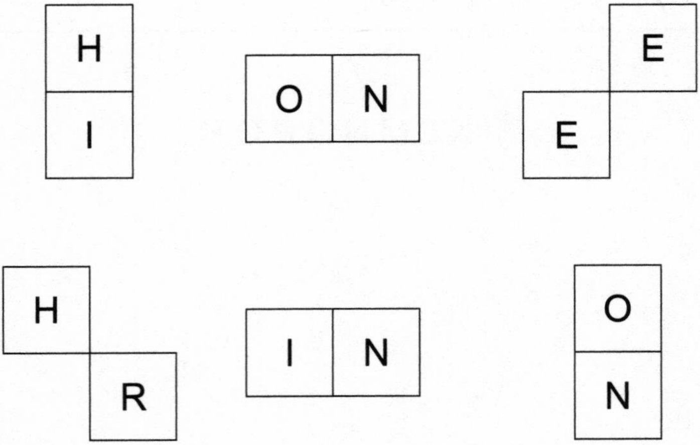

SENTENCE MAKER 2

Make up a sentence with words that fit into the structures given, where C stands for Consonant, and V stands for Vowel.

For example the sentence SHE LIKES CATS would fit into the structure CCV CVCVC CVCC. Proper nouns are allowed, and you can put punctuation anywhere in the sentence if you would like to.

V ______________________________

C V C V ______________________________

V C ______________________________

C V C ______________________________

C V C C ______________________________

WORKING IT OUT 2

Work out what these phrases have in common.

Bob Lovell says Eunice demanded toast yesterday.

Wow! Remember that classic rumor?

Did Norman erase Steve's blurb?

Mom detected strangers going onto local steeples.

Dad thought that ships dredged landfill.

Level 2

SYLLABLE WORDS 2

The words to find each have 3 syllables. The last syllable or section of one word forms the first syllable or section of the next, for example WONDERFUL and FULFILLING.

Starting in the centre, draw a continuous line from one word to the next. There are four words to find.

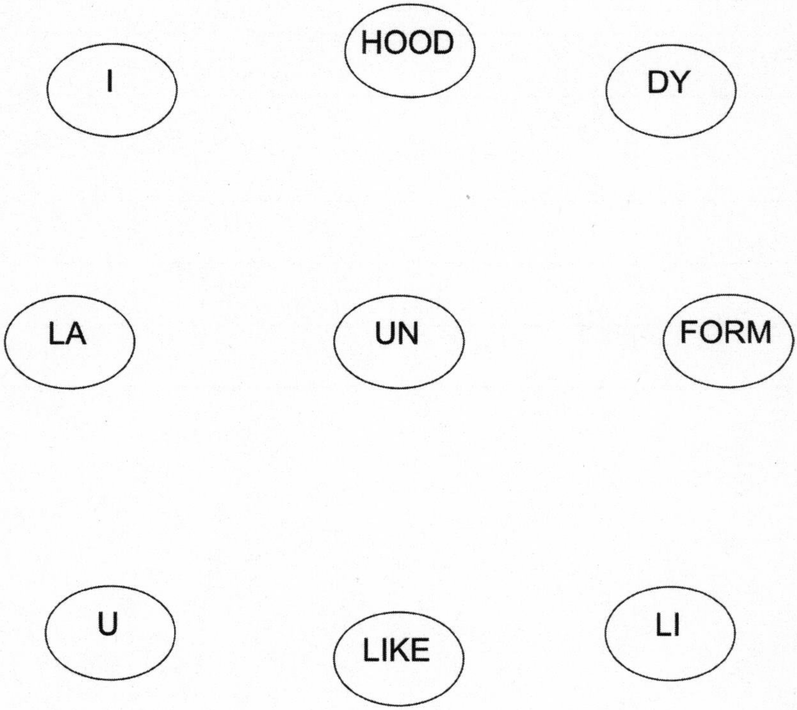

POETRY 2

Make up a poem with two stanzas of four lines each, where the second and fourth lines in each stanza rhyme.

The first line is given:

I love my teacher very much

MISSING LETTERS 2

Two letters are missing from each set of words. They are different letters for each set of words. What are the letters?

SET 1

__AME__

S__O__D

__ __EAR

UN__ __E

SET 2

__ARME__

S__O__D

__ __EAK

UNA__A__E

WORD TRAIL 2

Find the 6 words listed in the grid starting with the circled letter. The last letter of one word forms the first letter of the next word.

Words go horizontally backward or forwards, or vertically upwards or downwards.

G	A	L	O	C
E	(L)	I	L	A
L	O	B	E	L
A	Y	A	L	E
L	E	B	E	V

LOYAL

LEGAL

LIBEL

LOCAL

LEVEL

LABEL

THREE LETTERS 2

How many words can you think of that contain the three given letters in this order? They do not need to be together in the word, can occur anywhere, but need to be in this order. For example if the letters were ITE, the words could be ITEm; bITE, InnovaTE, sIsTEr, and so on.

Aim to avoid proper nouns.

You have two options here. You can spend one minute on each set of three letters, or you can choose one set of letters and spend five minutes on it.

S T R	
O U S	
R E E	
E A N	
A C K	

LETTER SWAP 2

Three letters in each phrase have been swapped. Can you work out which three you can swap back to make another sentence. For example in the sentence <u>C</u>ORY <u>W</u>OULD <u>T</u>ALK, the letters C, W and T can be swapped to form <u>T</u>ORY <u>C</u>OULD <u>W</u>ALK.

HE WOVE YOUR LOUSE

IT'S SMOKING BY TRAIN

Level 3

ROWS AND COLUMNS 3

Fill in the column with a word that makes the rows into complete words. There are no proper nouns used. There may be more than one answer.

S		A	Y
D		L	L
S		I	N
W		S	E
I		E	D

CONCENTRATION 3

SEQUENCE 1 Which of the sequences is the mirror image of:

V T H I O Y X M A M O X H I A

1. A I H X O M A M X Y I O H T V
2. A I X H O M A M X Y O I H T V
3. A I H X O M A X M Y O I H T V
4. A I H X O M M A X Y O I H T V
5. A I H O X M A M X Y O I H T V
6. A I H X O M A M X Y O I H T V

SEQUENCE 2 Which of the sequences is the mirror image of:

a I H x O M a M X Y o I H t V

1. V t H I O Y X M a M O x H I a
2. V t H I o Y x M a M O x H I a
3. V t H I o Y X M a M O x H I a
4. V t H I o Y X M A M O x H I a
5. V t H I o Y X M a M O X H I a
6. V t h I o Y X M a M O x H I a

VOWEL WORDS 3

Choose words that fit the categories and include the given vowel.

The vowel can be used as often as you like in the word, but it must be the only vowel used.

Vowel: **I**	
Two boys' names	
Two girls' names	
One place name	
Two creatures' names	
Two types of food	
Two items of clothing	
A hobby or pastime	

CONTINUOUS WORDS 3

This is a list of words that have been joined together. Put the spaces in the appropriate places to work out the list of words.

BLUSHAMUSESHRUBBUSBUSHRUBBISHSHIRERUS-
ESUREBERRYYESRUSHBURSARYMARRYRASHSHAR
EEARAREASHAMSHAMEMESHSHEBRUISERISERUBY
BRAYYEARYAMABUSEARMYASSUMEBEERBRUSHME
RRYSUBURB

WORD IN WORD 3

Put the 4-letter words on the left hand side into the correct spaces to make 8-letter words.

RINK ROWS RUNE RAGS RANK RING	B					I	N	G
	D					T	E	R
	C					I	N	G
	D					I	L	Y
	B					T	T	E
	C					L	E	D

Level 3

WORD RHYME 3

Find as many words as you can that rhyme with the given word. Use a timer, and take a minute for each of the five words. Note that different words rhyme in different accents, so choose words that rhyme in your accent. Decide if you want to include proper nouns or not. You can include rhyming words with different spellings, for example REED and READ.

SHOUT	
YOU	
WHEN	
THIS	
COAL	

HALF WORDS 3

Join two half words together to form six lots of 6-letter words.

R	E	S		R	E	F
P	E	S		P	E	R
T	E	L		U	R	E
U	S	E		I	L	L
A	L	L		T	L	E
E	L	L		P	A	S

1. ____________________

2. ____________________

3. ____________________

4. ____________________

5. ____________________

6. ____________________

Level 3

X WORDS 3

Place the correct words in the rows in the grid so that both diagonals spell a four-letter word reading from top to bottom.

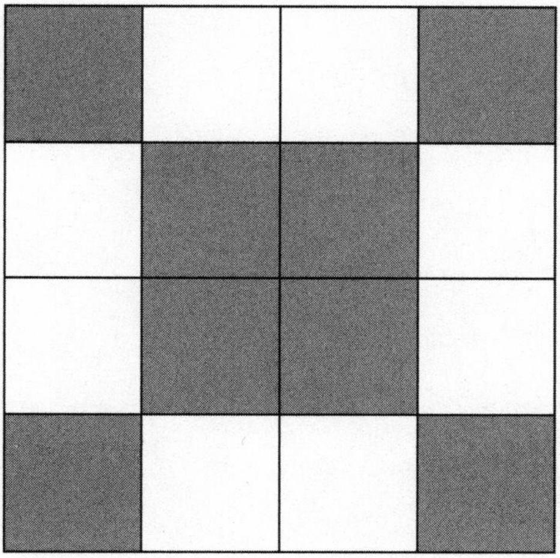

SHOW

DRAW

ANON

SNIP

ALPHABET TEASERS 3

P

Find the names of 10 fruits and vegetables starting with P

S

Find 10 words with the structure:

S + vowel + vowel + consonant

Level 3

ANAGRAM GRID 3

Solve the anagrams and place them into the correct spaces in the grid. One letter has been placed for you.

CHARN

THECA

THECA

HERCE

I LIKE … 3

All the items *'I like'* have a connection that the items *'I don't like'* do not have. Can you work out the connection?

I LIKE ...	... BUT I DON'T LIKE
Asia	Oceania
high	low
Eve	Adam
chic	sophisticated
going	coming
window	door
shoes	boots
minim	crotchet

Level 3

WORD FLOW 3

Think of five 5-letter words that start with the letters on the left and end with the letter in the middle. Then think of five 5-letter words that start with the letter in the middle and end with the letters on the right. Avoid using proper nouns.

For words ending in ‘S’ avoid using plurals, though verbs forms ending in ‘s’ are OK.

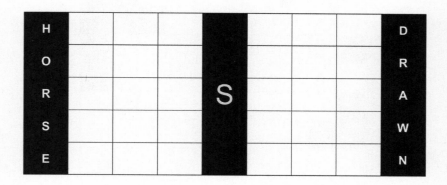

H								D
O								R
R				S				A
S								W
E								N

RHYME TIME 3

Each row in the grid contains two words that rhyme—an adjective and a noun.

Solve the clues then slot the words into the grid so that the gray column also contains two rhyming words.

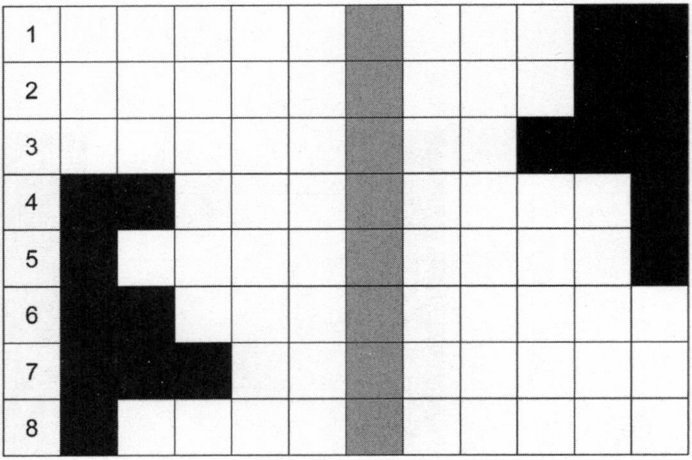

CLUES

1 VERDANT VEGETABLE SEED 5,4

2 RIDICULOUS FLOWER 5,4

3 BORING SEA BIRD 4,4

4 PLEASANT GRAIN 4,4

5 WET ENVELOPE ADDITION 4,5

6 WEALTHY CRONE 4,5

7 UNHURRIED BIRD 4,4

8 UNTETHERED LARGE ANIMAL 5,5

Level 3

MEMORY CIRCLE 3

Study the grid, and remember the shapes, the words and where they are positioned. Then turn the page and answer the questions.

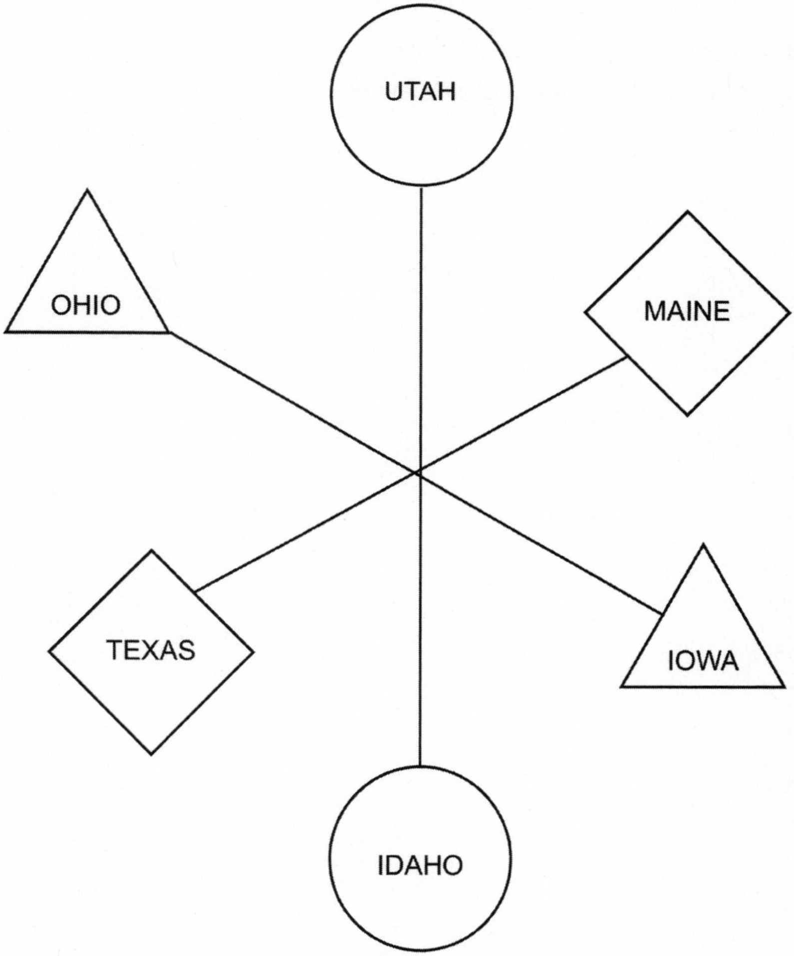

MEMORY CIRCLE 3

Questions

1. How many states have two syllables?
2. Name the states in the diamond shapes
3. Which state is opposite UTAH?
4. Which states is in the north west position?
5. Which state is between MAINE and IDAHO?

WORD CREATION 3

Taking the last letter of a 3-letter word, use it as the first letter of a new 3-letter word. For example the word after HAT may be TAR. Don't repeat words and avoid using proper nouns.

Within 5 minutes can you create at least 70 words?

NOW				
				70 words!

VOLVOGRAMS 3

Volvograms are words that spell another word when read backwards, for example BIN and NIB. Work out each pair of volvograms from the clues given, and then slot them into the crossword grid.

Reserve vehicle (3) (3)		
God of love, hurt (4) (4)		
Get lively and noisy over a handle (5) (5)		

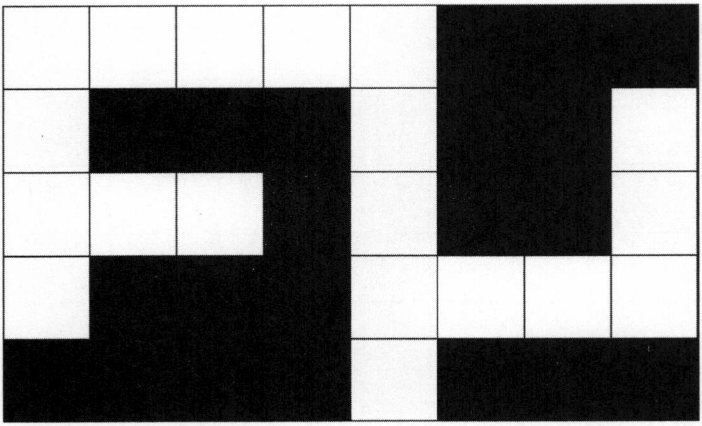

TRIANGLES 3

Each triangle contains a 3-letter, 4-letter and 5-letter word, placed in the direction of the arrows. Put the words into the correct triangles.

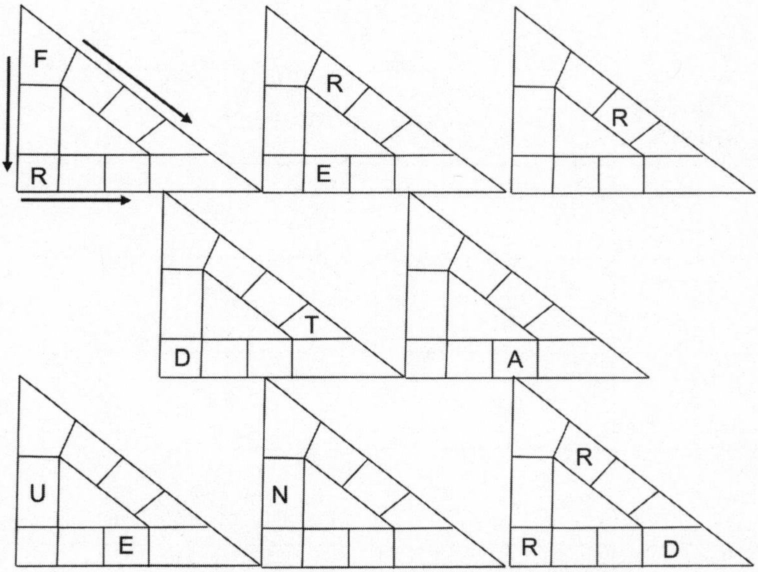

3-letter words	4-letter words	5-letter words
EBB	BATH	EARTH
END	BEAR	ENTER
FUR	DASH	FIELD
FUN	DEAR	FLASK
HAD	NECK	HEATH
HOB	NEED	HOVER
TAN	REED	TRACK
TAR	RISK	TREND

NINE WORDS 3

Write one or more complete sentences with words the same length as the first nine digits of the number pi (π): 3.14159265

No. of letters	Sentence
3	
1	
4	
1	
5	
9	
2	
6	
5	

MARRIED WITH CHILDREN 3

Take 2 letters from each parent's name and combine them to form a 4-letter name of their child. The (m) or (f) indicates the gender. There may be more than one answer.

GARY & ERIN (f)	
LUKE & TINA (m)	
JEFF & NULA (f)	
CARL & INGE (m)	

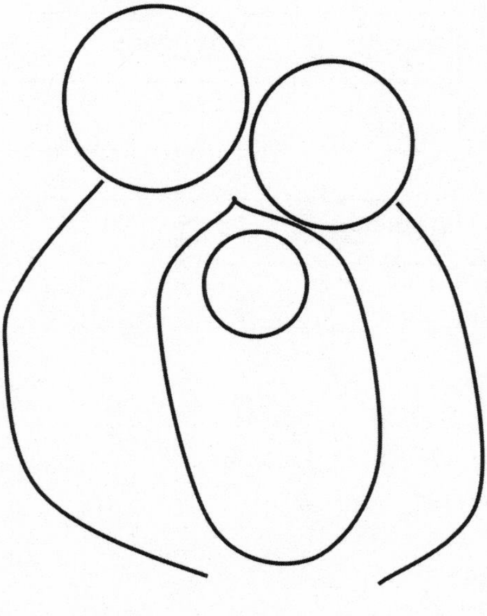

LETTER CHANGE 3

Change one letter in each of the four words so that they belong to a group of similar words. The letter to change has been underlined.

FLIPPER	MOCK	BOAT	SHOW

EAR	VAT	TRACK	BUN

SHOW	WINE	SHEET	GAIN

BRINE	RANG	GLOOM	VEIN

WHITE	BETTER	PET	IRK

DIAMOND WORDS 3

Find 11 words that fit the diamond grid. Avoid using the same word more than once, and words that are proper nouns.

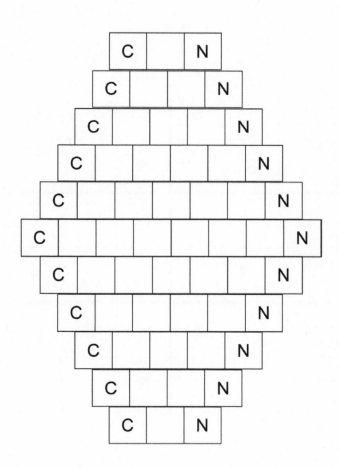

C		N					
C			N				
C				N			
C					N		
C						N	
C							N
C						N	
C					N		
C				N			
C			N				
C		N					

MINI WORD SUDOKU 3

Place the letters from the 6-letter word SCRIBE in the grid so that each column, each row, and each of the six 2×3 sub-grids contains all of the 6 letters from the word.

I		S	C		
	B		S		
C					
					R
		E		S	
		I	B		C

LETTER SHUFFLE 3

A saying has been placed in the grid in a continuous string, going from left to right, and reading from top to bottom. The 7 letters in the shaded squares have been rearranged.

The word lengths are: 4, 2, 3, 6, 4, 2, 3, 6

L	I	F	S	I
S	T	E	E	S
C	L	O	O	L
H	O	V	E	H
S	T	H	I	L
E	S	E	O	N

Saying:

___

___

___

SPEED WORDS 3

Choose 10 words that fit the criteria given. Choose words that are not proper nouns. Use a different word for each question.

Choose a word that:		
1	Rhymes with 'CARROT'	
2	Has 5 letters and ends with a double letter	
3	Has 2 syllables and starts with 'Q'	
4	Has 5 letters, 3 of which are vowels	
5	Starts with 'STR' and has 2 syllables	
6	Has 1 syllable and rhymes with 'SHONE'	
7	Has 2 syllables and ends with 'LT'	
8	Has 5 letters with 'V' in the middle	
9	Has 3 syllables and ends with 'CLE'	
10	Starts with 'M', ends with 'D' and contains a double letter	

LETTER BOXES 3

Take one letter from each box to form a 4-letter word. Topic: Food

R M C F	I O I E	C A S R	N H T E

CLUES 3

Solve the clues then find the letters, which are placed randomly in the grid. Cross them off, circle them, or color in the square as you find them.

CLUES

1. Begin (5)
2. Cheery and bright (5)
3. Loose (5)
4. Reduce the length (7)
5. Feeling of support (8)

T	Y	U	S	S
N	N	T	S	Y
S	H	A	P	E
Y	H	A	T	R
N	T	S	K	M
C	A	R	O	L

WORD PLUS WORD 3

Add a 3-letter word to the initial letter so that it also makes a 4-letter word, for example A + HEM. Make each of the 3-letter words different. Avoid using plurals and proper nouns.

V			
W			
X			
Y			
Z			

Add a 4-letter word to the initial letter so that it also makes a 5-letter word, for example A + CORN. Make each of the 4-letter words different. Avoid using plurals and proper nouns.

A				
B				
C				
D				
E				

SQUIDS 3

Can you place the letters in the correct squares so that the grid makes 4 words that read both horizontally and vertically?

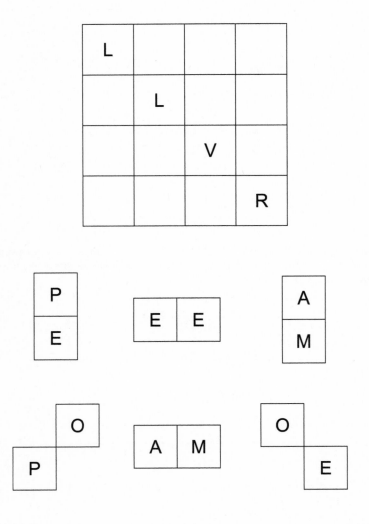

L			
	L		
		V	
			R

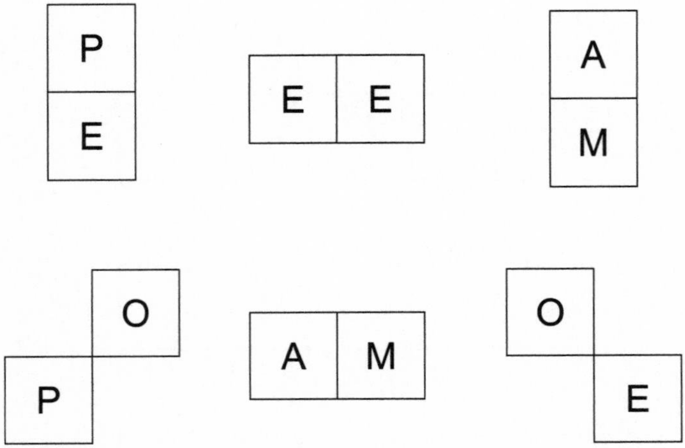

MISSING ALPHABET 3

There are 8 words, each having a different letter of the alphabet missing. Work out which letter goes in each word. None of the words are proper nouns.

The letters are provided so you can cross off each one as you find it.

QUI_	_AND	TA_I
HI_E		PO_T
EAR	HEN	ROIER

STUVWXYZ

SENTENCE MAKER 3

Make up a sentence with words that fit into the structures given, where C stands for Consonant, and V stands for Vowel.

For example the sentence SHE LIKES CATS would fit into the structure CCV CVCVC CVCC. Proper nouns are allowed, and you can put punctuation anywhere in the sentence if you would like to.

C V V C ____________________

C V C ____________________

C V V C V ____________________

V C ____________________

C C V V C ____________________

WORKING IT OUT 3

Work out what these phrases have in common.

Can Nina accept that tonight's show will lower ratings?

Who organized Dougie's sport tournament?

It's surely your responsibility; you understand data, apparently.

Although he exceeded Donna's success, she earned double everyone's salary.

Women never reach high hopes satisfactorily.

SYLLABLE WORDS 3

The words to find each have 3 syllables. The last syllable or section of one word forms the first syllable or section of the next, for example WONDERFUL and FULFILLING.

Starting in the centre, draw a continuous line from one word to the next. There are four words to find.

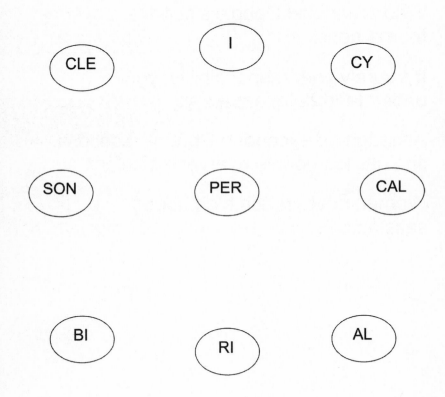

CLE I CY

SON PER CAL

BI RI AL

POETRY 3

This time make up a poem with two stanzas of four lines each, where the second and fourth lines in each stanza rhyme, as well as the first and third lines. Example:

My favorite color's *red*

Though sometimes it is *blue*

I may wear pink *instead*

When out of public *view*.

The first line is given:

I wish I had a cat

MISSING LETTERS 3

Two letters are missing from each set of words. They are different letters for each set of words. What are the letters?

SET 1

S _ E E _

_ A _ R E D

T _ R E A _

M I G _ _

SET 2

S _ E E _

_ A R E _

C O _ E _

S _ A _ E

WORD TRAIL 3

Find the 6 words listed in the grid starting with the circled letter. The last letter of one word forms the first letter of the next word.

Note that words can also go diagonally as well as horizontally backward or forwards, or vertically upwards or downwards.

V	I	C	U	B
I	C	I	C	I
(C)	O	M	Y	N
N	O	L	O	I
I	C	I	C	C

CIVIC
CONIC
COLIC
COMIC
CUBIC
CYNIC

THREE LETTERS 3

How many words can you think of that contain the three given letters in this order? They do not need to be together in the word, can occur anywhere, but need to be in this order. For example if the letters were ITE, the words could be ITEm; bITE, InnovaTE, sIsTEr, and so on.

Aim to avoid proper nouns.

You have two options here. You can spend one minute on each set of three letters, or you can choose one set of letters and spend five minutes on it.

S H E	
O T E	
I E T	
A L L	
S S E	

LETTER SWAP 3

Three letters in each phrase have been swapped. Can you work out which three you can swap back to make another sentence. For example in the sentence CORY WOULD TALK, the letters C, W and T can be swapped to form TORY COULD WALK.

TO NOW DISCUSS DITCHES

DON'T LOVE YOUR SLACK GLOBES

Level 4

ROWS AND COLUMNS 4

Fill in the column with a word that makes the rows into complete words. There are no proper nouns used. There may be more than one answer.

M	E		S
M	E		D
M	E		T
M	E		K
M	E		E

CONCENTRATION 4

SEQUENCE 1 Which of the sequences is the upside down version of:

E N E N O J R A W A K Y C H L

SEQUENCE 2 Which of the sequences is the upside down version of:

R K I e D I a N E D F r f E C

VOWEL WORDS 4

Choose words that fit the categories and include the given vowel.

The vowel can be used as often as you like in the word, but it must be the only vowel used.

Vowel: **O**	
Two boys' names	
Two girls' names	
Two place name	
Two creatures' names	
Two types of food	
Two items of clothing	
A hobby or pastime	

CONTINUOUS WORDS 4

This is a list of words that have been joined together. Put the spaces in the appropriate places to work out the list of words.

GRANDALARMHALLLAMPHAYGALAHARMMANY-
GLANDPAPAYAGANGPARAGRAPHGALLGAPPALMPAN
LANDLLAMAPAGANGLADMAYPANGLAGHAPPYPRAYR
ANGHARPMALLPLAYPARRYHANGARPALLPLANHAND
PANDA

WORD IN WORD 4

Put the 4-letter words on the left hand side into the correct spaces to make 8-letter words.

	S					E	L	Y
PANG	S					I	N	G
MALL								
MOOT	S					E	S	T
PILL								
PILL	S					H	L	Y
TACK								
EVER	S					L	E	D
	S					A	G	E

WORD RHYME 4

Find as many words as you can that rhyme with the given word. Use a timer, and take a minute for each of the five words. Note that different words rhyme in different accents, so choose words that rhyme in your accent. Decide if you want to include proper nouns or not. You can include rhyming words with different spellings, for example REED and READ.

KING	
GREEN	
HAY	
CHECK	
ALL	

HALF WORDS 4

Join two half words together to form six lots of 6-letter words.

G	L	E		A	C	E
P	E	N		K	E	N
T	A	C		T	I	C
C	I	A		A	C	A
K	L	E		A	W	A
C	I	L		T	A	N

1. ____________________________
2. ____________________________
3. ____________________________
4. ____________________________
5. ____________________________
6. ____________________________

X WORDS 4

Place the correct words in the rows in the grid so that both diagonals spell a four-letter word reading from top to bottom.

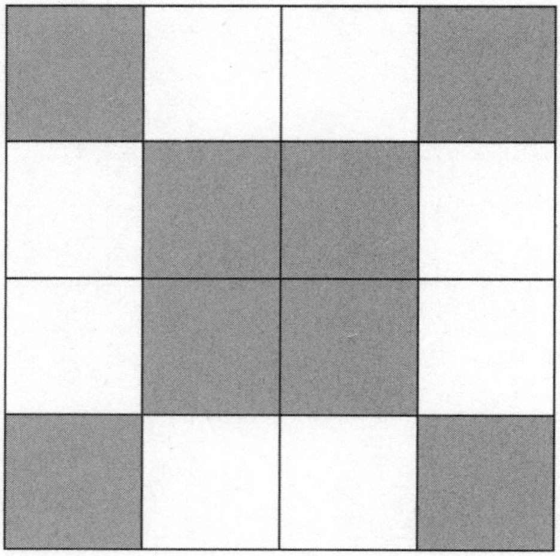

SNUB

KALE

SLIM

BUMP

ALPHABET TEASERS 4

M

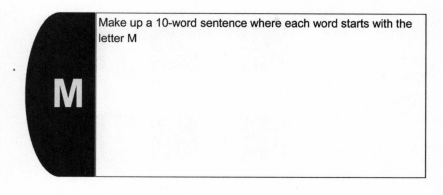

Make up a 10-word sentence where each word starts with the letter M

V

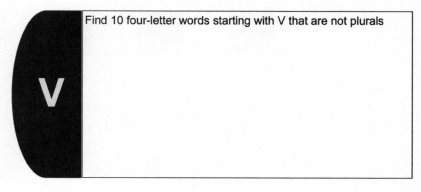

Find 10 four-letter words starting with V that are not plurals

ANAGRAM GRID 4

Solve the anagrams and place them into the correct spaces in the grid. One letter has been placed for you.

LODUC

DUCLO

SUCLO

LOOSS

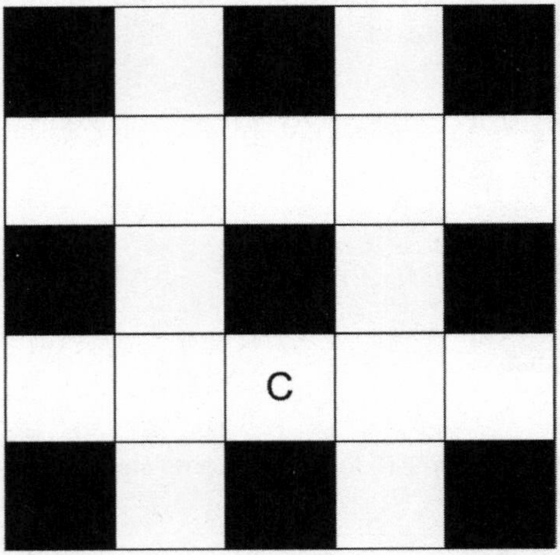

Level 4

I LIKE ... 4

All the items *'I like'* have a connection that the items *'I don't like'* do not have. Can you work out the connection?

I LIKE ...	... BUT I DON'T LIKE
banana	strawberry
dividing	multiplying
serene	peaceful
tomorrow	yesterday
Abraham	Moses
untruthful	inaccurate
protocol	procedures
cheese	meat

WORD FLOW 4

Think of five 5-letter words that start with the letters on the left and end with the letter in the middle. Then think of five 5-letter words that start with the letter in the middle and end with the letters on the right. Avoid using proper nouns.

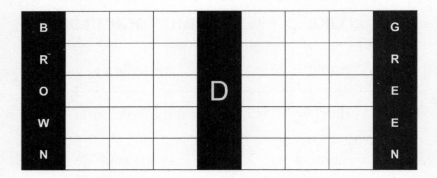

B								G
R								R
O				D				E
W								E
N								N

Level 4

RHYME TIME 4

Each row in the grid contains two words that rhyme—an adjective and a noun.

Solve the clues then slot the words into the grid so that the gray column also contains two rhyming words.

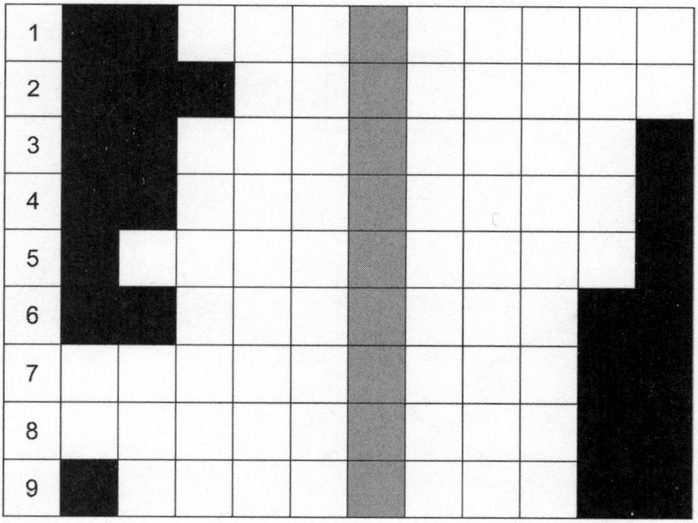

CLUES

1 MILD GRANULES 5,4

2 SAD FRIEND 4,4

3 THIN SONG 4,4

4 PLAIN CRUSTACEAN 4,4

5 FANTASTIC PAL 5,4

6 ROSY TOP 3,4

7 STINGY RULER 4,5

8 SUPERIOR FLESH 5,4

9 FEEBLE BILL 4,4

MEMORY CIRCLE 4

Study the grid, and remember the shapes, the words and where they are positioned. Then turn the page and answer the questions.

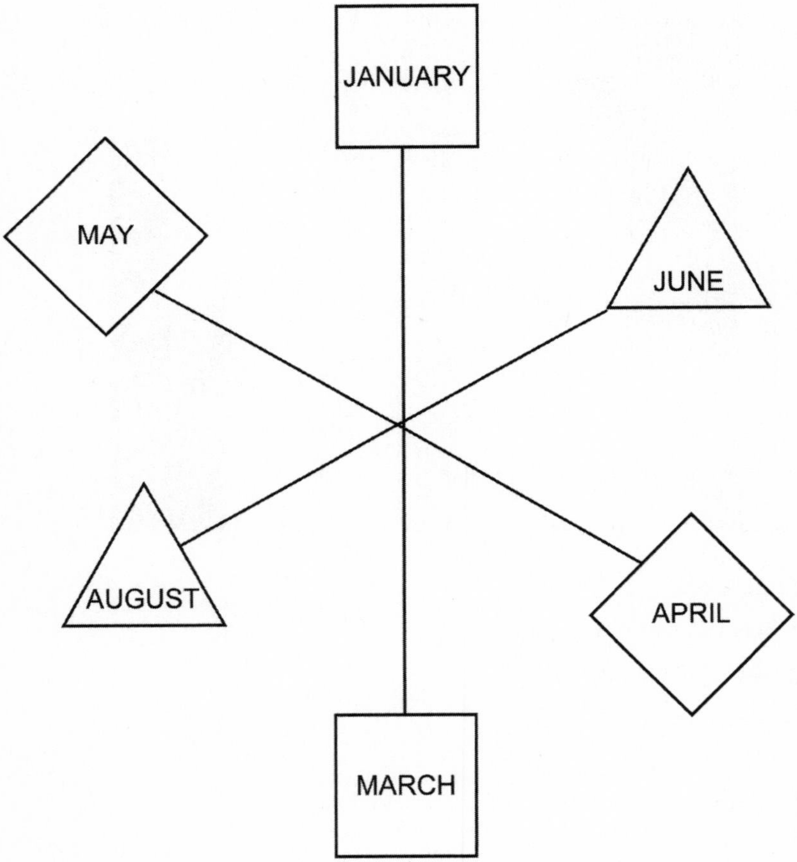

MEMORY CIRCLE 4

Questions

1. Name the months in triangles
2. Which month is in the south east position?
3. Going in a clockwise direction, which month is 3 spaces after MARCH?
4. Which month is opposite APRIL?
5. Which months are missing?

WORD CREATION 4

Taking the **last** letter of a word, use it as the **first** letter of a new word of any length. NOTE: All words can only contain the **vowel 'E'**. For example the word after HEEL may be LEVER. Don't repeat words and avoid using proper nouns. Within 5 minutes can you create at least 55 words?

SHEET				
				55 words!

VOLVOGRAMS 4

Volvograms are words that spell another word when read backwards, for example BIN and NIB. Work out each pair of volvograms from the clues given, and then slot them into the crossword grid.

Married droplets (3) (3)

See how long it takes to send (4) (4)

Unearthed cotton fabric (5) (5)

TRIANGLES 4

Each triangle contains a 3-letter, 4-letter and 5-letter word, placed in the direction of the arrows. Put the words into the correct triangles.

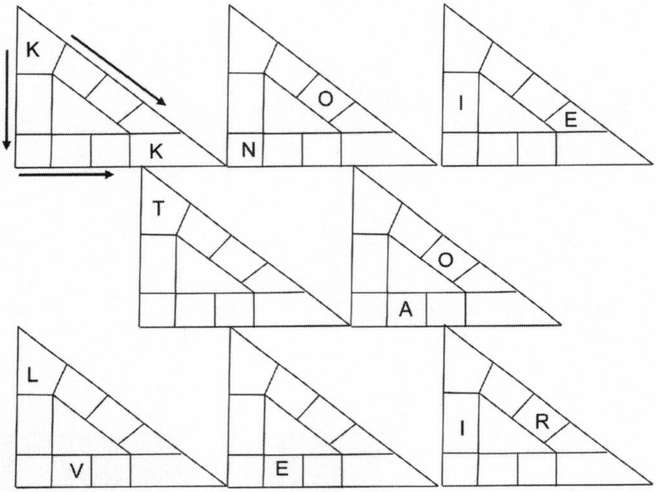

3-letter words	4-letter words	5-letter words
KEY	EASE	KAYAK
KIN	EVER	KNOWS
LIE	NECK	LARGE
LIP	NETS	LIVER
SPY	PAVE	SNACK
SUN	PEAR	SNOWS
TIE	YAKS	TIGER
TIP	YANK	TITHE

NINE WORDS 4

Write one or more complete sentences with words containing 10 through to 2 letters.

No. of letters	Sentence
10	
9	
8	
7	
6	
5	
4	
3	
2	

MARRIED WITH CHILDREN 4

Take 2 letters from each parent's name and combine them to form a 4-letter name of their child. The (m) or (f) indicates the gender. There may be more than one answer.

DEAN & OLGA (m)	
EWEN & MAUD (f)	
HANS & JODY (m)	
JOEL & GAIL (f)	

Level 4

LETTER CHANGE 4

Change one letter in each of the four words so that they belong to a group of similar words. The letter to change has been underlined.

CHAIN	SEAS	SODA	CONCH

RHO	THERE	WHAM	SHY

US	DAWN	LIFT	FIGHT

PEAR	TRY	SON	WEEK

PLOY	SCONE	ART	STALE

DIAMOND WORDS 4

Find 11 words that fit the diamond grid. Avoid using the same word more than once, and words that are proper nouns.

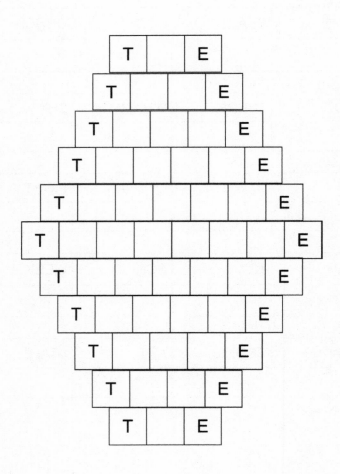

T		E					
T			E				
T				E			
T					E		
T						E	
T							E
T						E	
T					E		
T				E			
T			E				
T		E					

Level 4

MINI WORD SUDOKU 4

Place the letters from the 6-letter word **REASON** in the grid so that each column, each row, and each of the six 2×3 sub-grids contains all of the 6 letters from the word.

R		S	A		N
	E			R	
	N			S	
N		E	S		O

LETTER SHUFFLE 4

A saying has been placed in the grid in a continuous string, going from left to right, and reading from top to bottom. The 7 letters in the shaded squares have been rearranged.

The word lengths are: 4, 2, 4, 4, 2, 4, 2, 8

F	A	L	S	I
N	L	I	V	E
W	B	T	H	A
L	M	U	C	O
A	S	P	H	S
S	I	O	L	E

Saying:

____

____

____

SPEED WORDS 4

Choose 10 words that fit the criteria given. Choose words that are not proper nouns. Use a different word for each question.

Choose a word that:		
1	Has 3 'A's	
2	Has 5 syllables	
3	Has 12 letters	
4	Is a compound word ending with 'D'	
5	Contains the letters 'CK' twice	
6	Starts with 'E' and ends with 'ER'	
7	Is a compound word starting with 'L'	
8	Is an anagram of 'RASHELMS'	
9	Rhymes with 'DOWDY'	
10	Starts with 'L' and can prefix the word 'BERRY'	

LETTER BOXES 4

Take one letter from each box to form a 5-letter word. Topic: Fruit

M P M G L	A E E E R	M L N A A	P O C O G	O E N H N

CLUES 4

Solve the clues then find the letters, which are placed randomly in the grid. Cross them off, circle them, or color in the square as you find them.

CLUES

1. Monarch (5)
2. Fowl (7)
3. Head of government (9)
4. Brightly colored insect (9)

N	Y	S	H	E
E	E	E	B	C
Q	U	I	C	K
I	N	R	U	P
N	T	T	T	L
F	R	E	E	D

WORD PLUS WORD 4

Add a 4-letter word to the initial letter so that it also makes a 5-letter word, for example A + CORN. Make each of the 4-letter words different. Avoid using plurals and proper nouns.

F				
G				
H				
I				
J				
K				
P				
R				
S				
T				

MISSING ALPHABET 4

There are 8 words, each having a different letter of the alphabet missing. Work out which letter goes in each word. None of the words are proper nouns.

The letters are provided so you can cross off each one as you find it.

RIN_	HER_	L_CE
_ORE		WOR_
TON_	TRA_	K_TE

ACEGIKMO

SQUIDS 4

Can you place the letters in the correct squares so that the grid makes 4 words that read both horizontally and vertically?

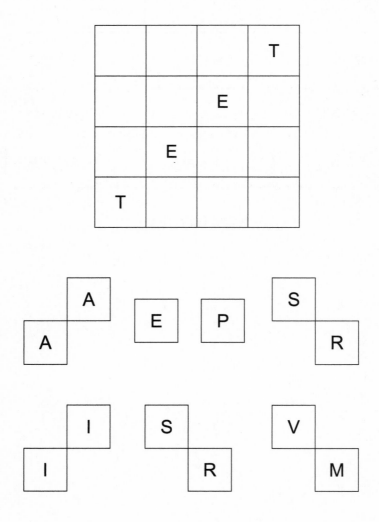

			T
		E	
	E		
T			

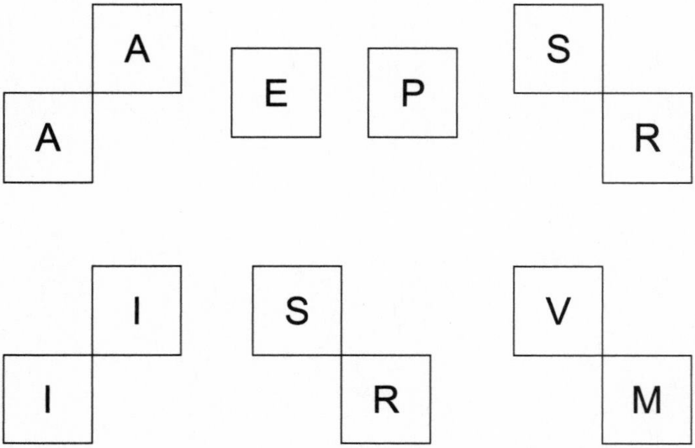

SENTENCE MAKER 4

Make up a sentence with words that fit into the structures given, where C stands for Consonant, and V stands for Vowel.

For example the sentence SHE LIKES CATS would fit into the structure CCV CVCVC CVCC. Proper nouns are allowed, and you can put punctuation anywhere in the sentence if you would like to.

C C V ______________________

C V C ______________________

C V C ______________________

V C ______________________

C C V ______________________

C V C ______________________

WORKING IT OUT 4

Work out what these phrases have in common.

"Mommy" called Eddie, "kitty's purring."

Tell Poppy I'll feel better soon.

Johnny's colleagues need three current notebooks.

"Mushroom pizza? Yummy food!" announced Bella.

"Thirteen million?" guessed Ann. "Approximately fourteen" added Jeff.

SYLLABLE WORDS 4

The words to find each have 3 syllables. The last syllable or section of one word forms the first syllable or section of the next, for example WONDERFUL and FULFILLING.

Starting in the centre, draw a continuous line from one word to the next. There are four words to find.

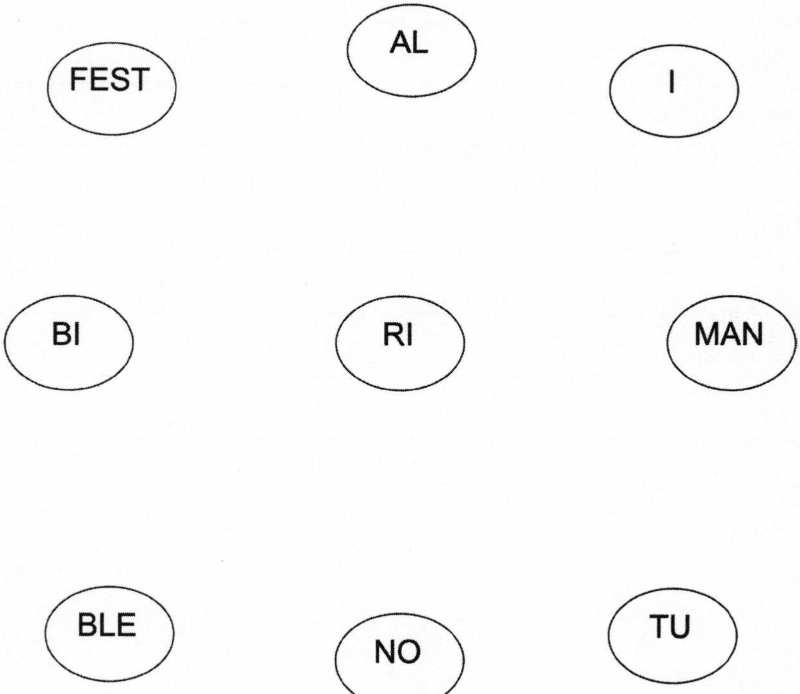

POETRY 4

Make up a poem with two stanzas of four lines each, where the second and fourth lines in each stanza rhyme, as well as the first and third lines. The first line is given:

I think I saw a rabbit

MISSING LETTERS 4

Two letters are missing from each set of words. They are different letters for each set of words. What are the letters?

SET 1

__ H __ I R

S __ A T __

__ W __ E D

S __ __ E L

SET 2

C __ __ I R

S __ __ WED

C __ __ RE

S __ __ AL

WORD TRAIL 4

Find the 6 words listed in the grid starting with the circled letter. The last letter of one word forms the first letter of the next word.

Note that words can go diagonally as well as horizontally backward or forwards, or vertically upwards or downwards.

A	M	L	P	H
L	O	(A)	A	O
O	R	A	N	R
A	H	A	E	T
P	N	E	R	A

ALPHA
AORTA
ARENA
AROMA
ALOHA
APNEA

THREE LETTERS 4

How many words can you think of that contain the three given letters in this order? They do not need to be together in the word, can occur anywhere, but need to be in this order. For example if the letters were ITE, the words could be ITEm; bITE, InnovaTE, sIsTEr, and so on.

Aim to avoid proper nouns.

You have two options here. You can spend one minute on each set of three letters, or you can choose one set of letters and spend five minutes on it.

S H E	
C U E	
O N G	
E T Y	
T T E	

LETTER SWAP 4

Three letters in each phrase have been swapped. Can you work out which three you can swap back to make another sentence. For example in the sentence CORY WOULD TALK, the letters C, W and T can be swapped to form TORY COULD WALK.

ELLA FIGHTS SIRES

I HAVE TEN RAGS, PAL

Level 5

ROWS AND COLUMNS 5

Fill in the column with a word that makes the rows into complete words. There are no proper nouns used. There may be more than one answer.

T	E		L
T	E		M
T	E		M
T	E		M
T	E		T

CONCENTRATION 5

SEQUENCE 1 Which of the sequences is the same as:

K I R B Y S T E E B A C E L A

1	2	3	4	5	6
K	A	K	A	K	A
I	L	I	L	I	L
R	E	R	E	R	E
B	C	B	C	B	C
Y	A	Y	A	Y	A
S	B	S	B	S	E
T	E	T	E	T	E
E	E	E	E	E	E
E	T	E	T	E	T
C	S	B	S	E	S
A	Y	A	Y	A	B
B	B	C	B	C	Y
E	I	L	R	E	R
L	R	L	I	L	I
A	K	A	K	A	K

CONCENTRATION 5, continued

SEQUENCE 2 Which of the sequences is the same as:

E R A e B T h T u O n u E G L

1	2	3	4	5	6
E	˥	E	˥	E	˥
R	⅁	R	⅁	R	⅁
A	Ǝ	a	Ǝ	A	Ǝ
e	n	e	n	e	∩
B	N	B	u	B	u
T	O	T	O	T	O
H	n	h	n	h	∩
T	⊥	T	⊥	T	⊥
u	ɥ	u	ɥ	u	ɥ
O	⊥	O	ʇ	O	⊥
n	ᗺ	n	ᗺ	n	ᗺ
u	ǝ	u	ǝ	u	Ǝ
E	∀	E	∀	E	∀
G	ᴚ	G	ᴚ	G	ᴚ
L	Ǝ	L	Ǝ	L	Ǝ

Level 5

VOWEL WORDS 5

Choose words that fit the categories and include the given vowel.

The vowel can be used as often as you like in the word, but it must be the only vowel used.

Vowel: **U**	
Two boys' names	
Two girls' names	
One place name	
Two creatures' names	
Two types of food	
An ethnic group	
A hobby or pastime	

CONTINUOUS WORDS 5

This is a list of words that have been joined together. Put the spaces in the appropriate places to work out the list of words.

SEVENDEPENDELDEREVENELEVENSENDLE-
PERNERVEPENREEDDEERREPELSEERLEVEELESSE
NPEELSEEDLEVELDRESSREDSERVESENSEPRESSN
EVERSEENSEVERRENDERSERENEPEEPSNEERVEE
RSPREEVENEERPEERVERSE

WORD IN WORD 5

Put the 4-letter words on the left hand side into the correct spaces to make 8-letter words.

MEND LIEN BAND MATE CHIN PERT	A					O	N	S
	A					U	R	S
	A					U	R	E
	A					A	T	E
	A					I	N	G
	A					G	L	Y

WORD RHYME 5

Find as many words as you can that rhyme with the given word. Use a timer, and take a minute for each of the five words. Note that different words rhyme in different accents, so choose words that rhyme in your accent. Decide if you want to include proper nouns or not. You can include rhyming words with different spellings, for example REED and READ.

ON	
KEY	
SNOW	
EYE	
LONG	

HALF WORDS 5

Join two half words together to form six lots of 6-letter words.

T	I	C		T	O	R
H	E	N		P	I	C
I	D	E		A	D	E
L	I	C		L	A	C
t	I	R		C	A	P
D	E	C		K	E	T

1. ______________________________

2. ______________________________

3. ______________________________

4. ______________________________

5. ______________________________

6. ______________________________

X WORDS 5

Place the correct words in the rows in the grid so that both diagonals spell a four-letter word reading from top to bottom.

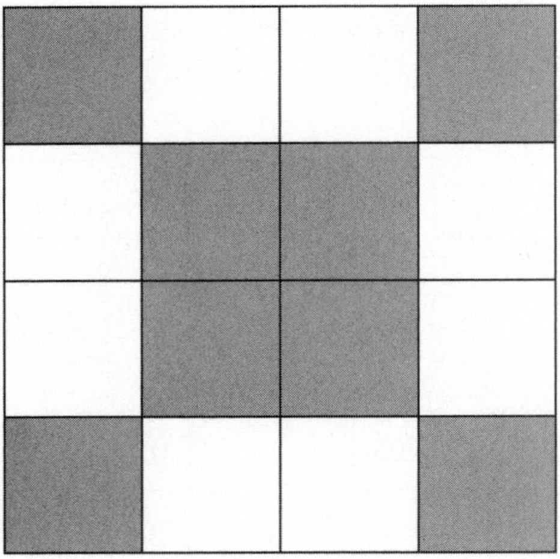

SHOP

SLAB

TRAP

TAIL

ALPHABET TEASERS 5

G

Find 10 words that contain GG

I

Find 10 girls' names starting with I

N

Find 10 adjectives beginning with N

ANAGRAM GRID 5

Solve the anagrams and place them into the correct spaces in the grid. One letter has been placed for you.

HARTS
HARES
SAREE
RATCH

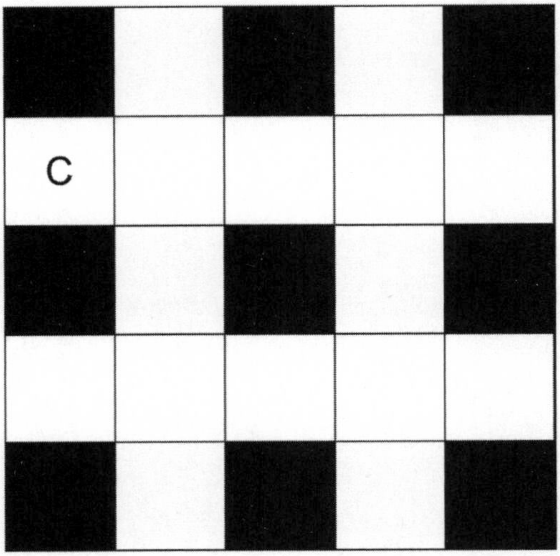

I LIKE ... 5

All the items *'I like'* have a connection that the items *'I don't like'* do not have. Can you work out the connection?

I LIKE ...	... BUT I DON'T LIKE
me	you
bath	shower
red	yellow
bags	luggage
hot	cool
fresh	stale
lamb	mutton
cars	vehicles

WORD FLOW 5

Think of five 5-letter words that start with the letters on the left and end with the letter in the middle. Then think of five 5-letter words that start with the letter in the middle and end with the letters on the right. Avoid using proper nouns.

S								M
P								O
E				H				N
N								E
D								Y

RHYME TIME 5

Each row in the grid contains two words that rhyme—an adjective and a noun.

Solve the clues then slot the words into the grid so that the gray column also contains two rhyming words.

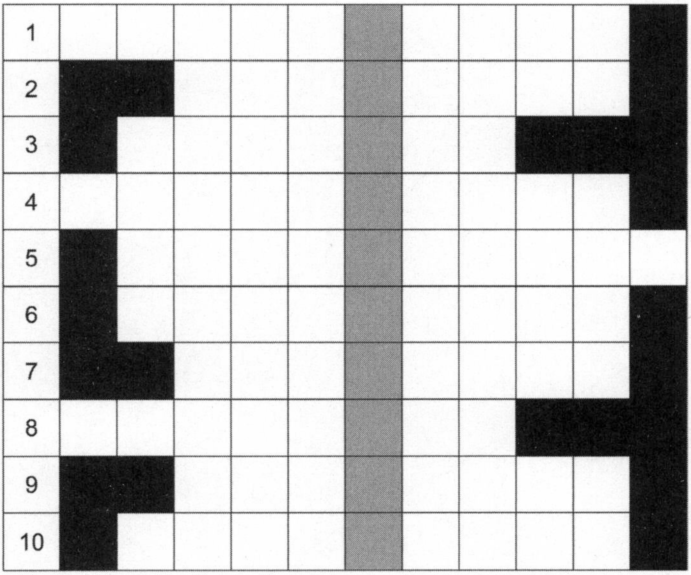

CLUES

1 UNDERHAND WIFE 5,5

2 BLOND TRESS 4,4

3 AWFUL BIRD 4,3

4 WEAK SEA CREATURE 5,5

5 UNADORNED METAL LINKS 5,5

6 UNCONTROLLABLE INFANT 4,5

7 GENUINE FOOD 4,4

8 ADORABLE FOOTWEAR 4,4

9 TARDY FLAKES 4,4

10 SPOTLESS YOUTH 5,4

MEMORY CIRCLE 5

Study the grid, and remember the shapes, the words and where they are positioned. Then turn the page and answer the questions.

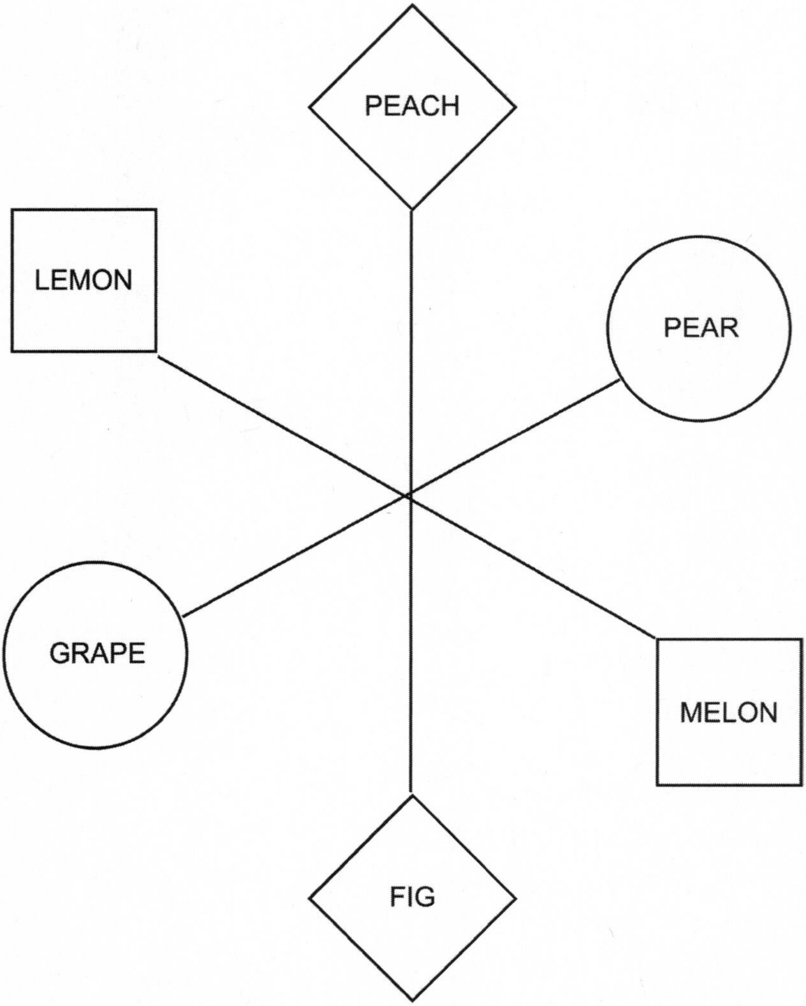

MEMORY CIRCLE 5

Questions

1. Name the fruits that contain the letter M
2. Which fruit is opposite PEAR?
3. Going in a clockwise direction, which fruit is 3 spaces after PEACH?
4. Name the 2 fruits that come between GRAPE and PEAR
5. Name the fruits in the circles

WORD CREATION 5

Taking the middle letter of a 5-letter word, use it as the first letter of a new 5-letter word. For example the word after HEATH may be ALTER. Don't repeat words and avoid using proper nouns. Within 5 minutes can you create at least 50 words?

LEVER				
				50 words!

VOLVOGRAMS 5

Volvograms are words that spell another word when read backwards, for example BIN and NIB. Work out each pair of volvograms from the clues given, and then slot them into the crossword grid.

Vegetable month (3) (3) ☐ ☐

Exchange feet (4) (4) ☐ ☐

Neat and tidy vehicles (5) (5) ☐ ☐

TRIANGLES 5

Each triangle contains a 3-letter, 4-letter and 5-letter word, placed in the direction of the arrows. Put the words into the correct triangles.

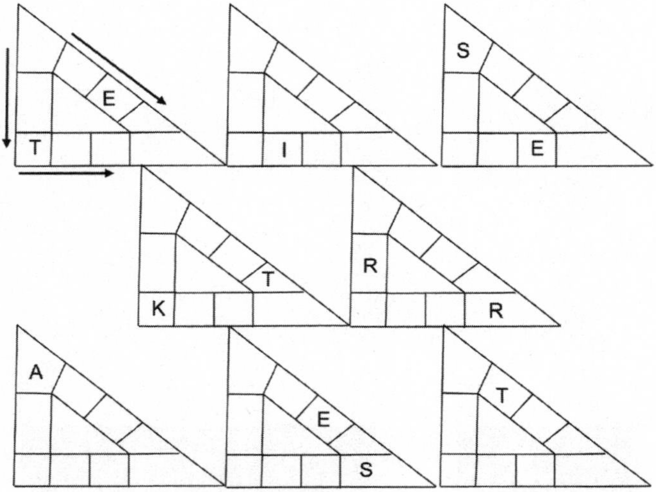

3-letter words	4-letter words	5-letter words
ARE	ABET	AMISS
ASK	AVER	ARISE
EAT	ELMS	EATER
ERA	EPEE	EVENT
INK	KISS	IRATE
IRE	KITE	ITEMS
SIT	TOUR	SMART
SPA	TOUT	STEER

NINE WORDS 5

Write one or more complete sentences using words of one syllable that only contain the vowel 'E'. There can be as many E's in the word as you like, but there must be no other vowels.

Sentence

MARRIED WITH CHILDREN 5

Take 2 letters from each parent's name and combine them to form a 4-letter name of their child. The (m) or (f) indicates the gender. There may be more than one answer.

DEAN & MIMI (f)	
WALT & IONA (m)	
JOHN & KATE (f)	
MIKE & RULA (m)	

LETTER CHANGE 5

Change one letter in each of the four words so that they belong to a group of similar words. The letter to change has been underlined.

FREE	BUSY	SHRUG	GLASS

CAKE	PONY	SEW	BANAL

EAT	DOE	BIND	WISH

MOW	SITTER	HUNT	GRAY

MAY	MEEK	MOUTH	NEAR

DIAMOND WORDS 5

Find 11 words that fit the diamond grid. Avoid using the same word more than once, and words that are proper nouns.

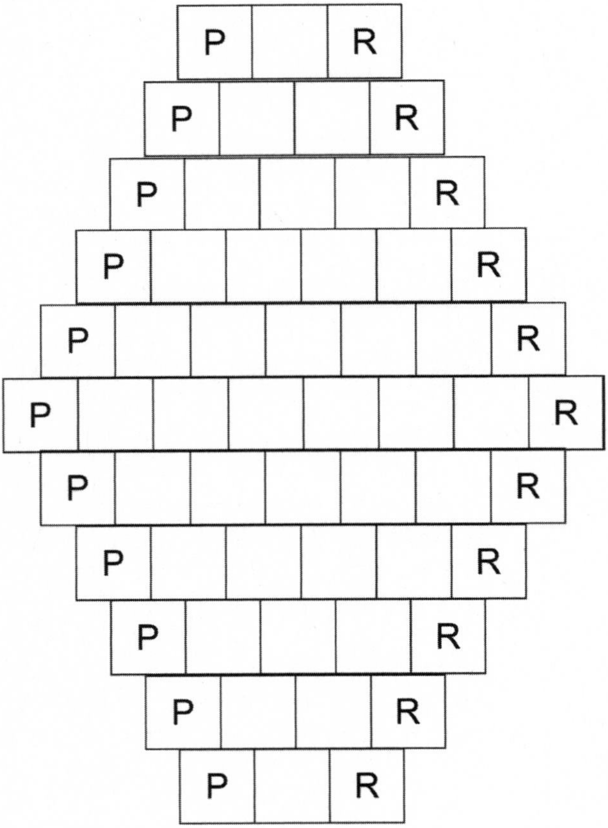

Level 5

MINI WORD SUDOKU 5

Place the letters from the 6-letter word KAIZEN in the grid so that each column, each row, and each of the six 2×3 sub-grids contains all of the 6 letters from the word.

		K			A
Z				K	I
					E
K					
E	N				K
I			A		

LETTER SHUFFLE 5

A saying has been placed in the grid in a continuous string, going from left to right, and reading from top to bottom. The 7 letters in the shaded squares have been rearranged.

The word lengths are: 3, 2, 2, 6, 2, 3, 5, 2, 5

A	I	M	B	O
B	E	O	U	M
B	Y	E	A	S
T	O	U	C	H
U	L	D	O	E
W	R	L	N	G

Saying:

____

____

____

SPEED WORDS 5

Choose 10 words that fit the criteria given. Choose words that are not proper nouns. Use a different word for each question.

Choose a word that:		
1	Rhymes with 'LAUNCH'	
2	Is an anagram of 'BINARY'	
3	Has 7 letters with 'Q' in the middle	
4	Fits into Q _ _ _ G _	
5	Starts with 'U' and ends with 'Y'	
6	Is a compound word where both parts start with 'B'	
7	Ends with 'E' and is a suffix to the word 'SUN'	
8	Has the structure: vowel consonant vowel vowel	
9	Has 6 letters with 'FF' in the middle	
10	Starts with 'CHR' and isn't a proper noun	

LETTER BOXES 5

Take one letter from each box to form a 5-letter word. Topic: Animals

T B T C L	A A I I E	G M P S M	O I E U E	L R R R N

Level 5

CLUES 5

Solve the clues then find the letters, which are placed randomly in the grid. Cross them off, circle them, or color in the square as you find them.

CLUES

1. Not dark (5)
2. 1950's dance (5)
3. Attractive (6)
4. Using physical force to cause harm (7)
5. Full of life (7)

T	T	T	T	T
V	I	V	Y	I
T	R	A	I	T
E	L	B	H	O
N	P	R	L	E
S	W	I	N	G

WORD PLUS WORD 5

Add a 4-letter word to the initial letter so that it also makes a 5-letter word, for example A + CORN. Make each of the 4-letter words different. Avoid using plurals and proper nouns.

L				
M				
N				
O				
U				
V				
W				
Y				

MISSING ALPHABET 5

There are 9 words, each having a different letter of the alphabet missing. Work out which letter goes in each word. None of the words are proper nouns.

The letters are provided so you can cross off each one as you find it.

_URY		RAS_		HAR_
_OIN		_RINE		_EFER
THIK		HEL_		TRA_

B D F H J L N P R

SQUIDS 5

Can you place the letters in the correct squares so that the grid makes 4 words that read both horizontally and vertically?

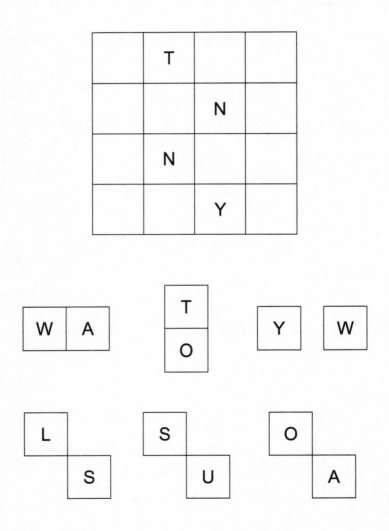

	T		
		N	
	N		
		Y	

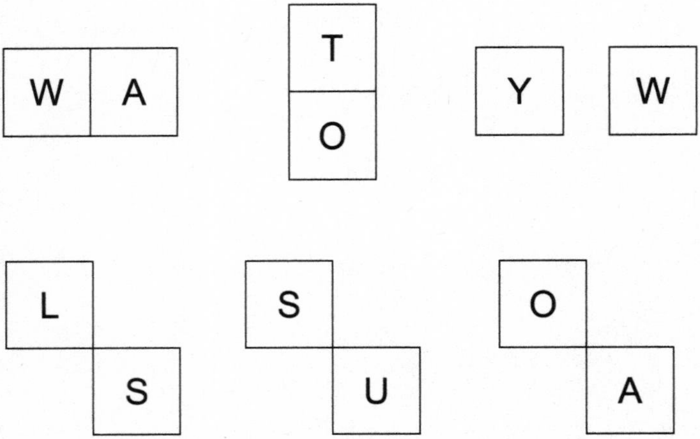

SENTENCE MAKER 5

Make up a sentence with words that fit into the structures given, where C stands for Consonant, and V stands for Vowel.

For example the sentence SHE LIKES CATS would fit into the structure CCV CVCVC CVCC. Proper nouns are allowed, and you can put punctuation anywhere in the sentence if you would like to.

C C V C ______________________________

C V C V ______________________________

C V C ______________________________

V ______________________________

C V C ______________________________

C V C C ______________________________

WORKING IT OUT 5

Work out what these phrases have in common.

YOU MAY HUM THAT.

THAT TWIT HIT HIM WITH MY HAT.

WHO AM I? I'M TAMMY.

"TOM, WAIT! A TAXI!"

OH, WHAT A HOAX, VIV.

SYLLABLE WORDS 5

The words to find each have 3 syllables. The last syllable or section of one word forms the first syllable or section of the next, for example WONDERFUL and FULFILLING.

Starting in the centre, draw a continuous line from one word to the next. There are four words to find.

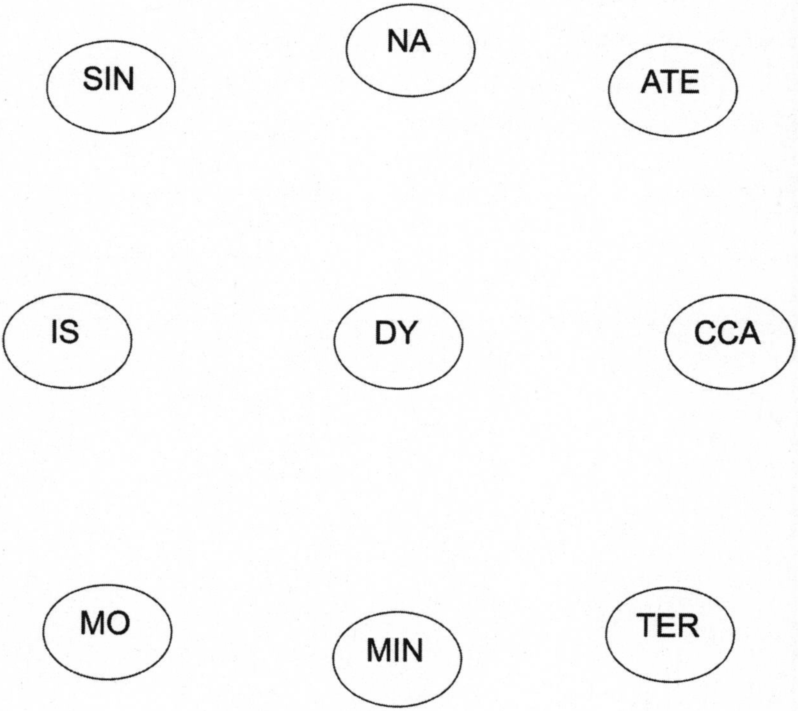

POETRY 5

Make up a traditional haiku.

Haiku are short poems originally developed by Japanese poets that often capture a feeling or image. They consist of 17 syllables, divided into three phrases: 5 syllables, 7 syllables, and 5 syllables. Example:

This is my daughter
For whom I have untold love
She lives in my heart.

Write a haiku that starts with the word:

Spring ____

____

____

MISSING LETTERS 5

Two letters are missing from each set of words. They are different letters for each set of words. What are the letters?

SET 1

B I __ O __

__ T O __ E

A __ C E __ T

__ W O R __

SET 2

B I __ O __

__ O A __

A __ E N __

A A E

WORD TRAIL 5

Find the 6 words listed in the grid starting with the circled letter. The last letter of one word forms the first letter of the next word.

Note that words can go diagonally as well as horizontally backward or forwards, or vertically upwards or downwards.

R	E	C	V	E
A	A	R	O	R
D	A	E	(R)	I
O	R	S	D	E
W	E	R	I	R

ROVER
RIDER
RISER
RACER
RADAR
ROWER

THREE LETTERS 5

How many words can you think of that contain the three given letters in this order? They do not need to be together in the word, can occur anywhere, but need to be in this order. For example if the letters were ITE, the words could be ITEm; bITE, InnovaTE, sIsTEr, and so on.

Aim to avoid proper nouns.

You have two options here. You can spend one minute on each set of three letters, or you can choose one set of letters and spend five minutes on it.

QUA	
NNE	
OOR	
DAY	
IDE	

LETTER SWAP 5

Three letters in each phrase have been swapped. Can you work out which three you can swap back to make another sentence. For example in the sentence C̲ORY W̲OULD T̲ALK, the letters C, W and T can be swapped to form T̲ORY C̲OULD W̲ALK.

SARA WAILS AT THE CATTLE

I BEAR TOYS AND CARS

Level 6

ROWS AND COLUMNS 6

Fill in the column with a word that makes the rows into complete words. There are no proper nouns used. There may be more than one answer.

C	O		T
C	O		Y
C	O		N
C	O		D
C	O		T

CONCENTRATION 6

Find this combination of words in the passage:

'June said that'

One day in July, June went to meet her friends Jane, Jude and Juno. June had said that it was good to meet with people in July, though Jane said that June was a better month. Juno said that June or July were both suitable. June said what she thought, and said that June wasn't a suitable month, while Jane said to herself 'Did June say that July was better just because Juno said that June was suitable?' June said to Juno that Jane said whatever came into her head, but Juno said that Jane said that she always thought out her answers before speaking. Jude said that June or July were never suitable and just because Juno said that they were, didn't make it so. June and Jude said that just because Jane and Juno were happy to meet in June, that didn't make it the most suitable option. "July is the better month" June said, "that is, without doubt, when we should meet." Juno said that she was happy; Jane said that she wasn't and Jude said that she didn't care and was going home.

VOWEL WORDS 6

Choose words that fit the categories and include the given vowels.

The vowels can only be used once in the word, and must be in this order. They can be together or separate.

Vowels: **AE**	
One boy's name	
One girl's name	
One place name	
One creature's name	
Two types of food	
One item of clothing	
A hobby or pastime	

CONTINUOUS WORDS 6

This is a list of words that have been joined together. Put the spaces in the appropriate places to work out the list of words.

BOLDDOLLOLDDONORBROOMLOOPBORONMOOD-
POLLDOORNOOKBORNPLODLOOMMONKBROOKDO
DOMOORLOOKMOONODDPORKBOOMNORMDROOP
PRODROOKPOLODOOMBOOKPOOLPROPDROOLRO
OMBOON

WORD IN WORD 6

Put the 4-letter words on the left hand side into the correct spaces to make 8-letter words.

LANK
HACK
RACK
LACE
PACE
RACE

S					L	E	D
S					M	A	N
S					L	E	T
S					T	O	N
S					E	R	S
S					B	O	S

Level 6

WORD RHYME 6

Find as many words as you can that rhyme with the given word. Use a timer, and take a minute for each of the five words. Note that different words rhyme in different accents, so choose words that rhyme in your accent. Decide if you want to include proper nouns or not. You can include rhyming words with different spellings, for example REED and READ.

SELL	
BACK	
FEED	
AIM	
SIZE	

HALF WORDS 6

Join two half words together to form six lots of 6-letter words.

A	L	S		A	C	I
E	S	S		E	L	S
I	D	E		A	D	E
B	L	E		A	S	S
L	A	B		S	T	A
D	I	C		D	E	C

1. ____

2. ____

3. ____

4. ____

5. ____

6. ____

X WORDS 6

Place the correct words in the rows in the grid so that both diagonals spell a five-letter word reading from top to bottom.

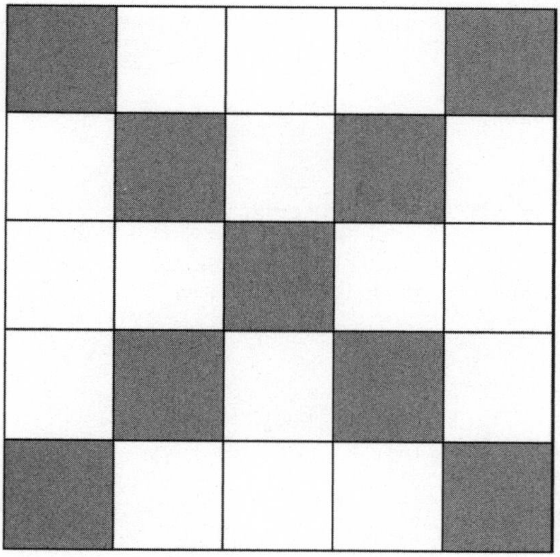

CLASS

EARTH

PRONG

BERRY

SPACE

ALPHABET TEASERS 6

E

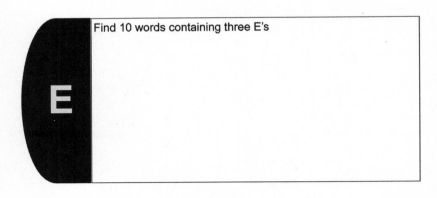

Find 10 words containing three E's

K

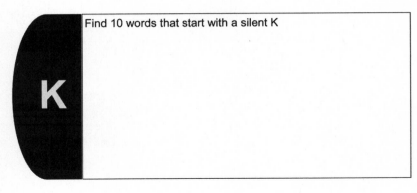

Find 10 words that start with a silent K

W

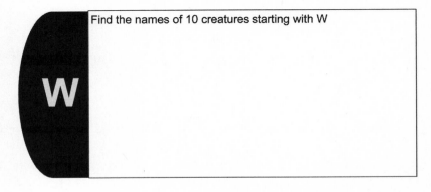

Find the names of 10 creatures starting with W

ANAGRAM GRID 6

Solve the anagrams and place them into the correct spaces in the grid.
Two letters have been placed for you.

TEARS
HATER
HATER
HASTE

I LIKE ... 6

All the items *'I like'* have a connection that the items *'I don't like'* do not have. Can you work out the connection?

I LIKE ...	... BUT I DON'T LIKE
calm	worry
cage	zoo
healed	torn
milk	quorn
game	sport
knife	spoon
babble	story
mine	yours

WORD FLOW 6

Think of four 6-letter words that start with the letters on the left and end with the letter in the middle. Then think of four 6-letter words that start with the letter in the middle and end with the letters on the right. Avoid using proper nouns.

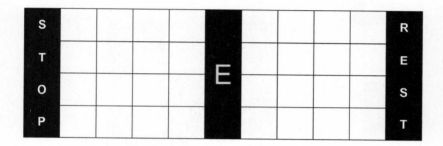

S										R
T					E					E
O										S
P										T

RHYME TIME 6

Each row in the grid contains two words that rhyme—an adjective and a noun.

Solve the clues then slot the words into the grid so that the gray column also contains two rhyming words.

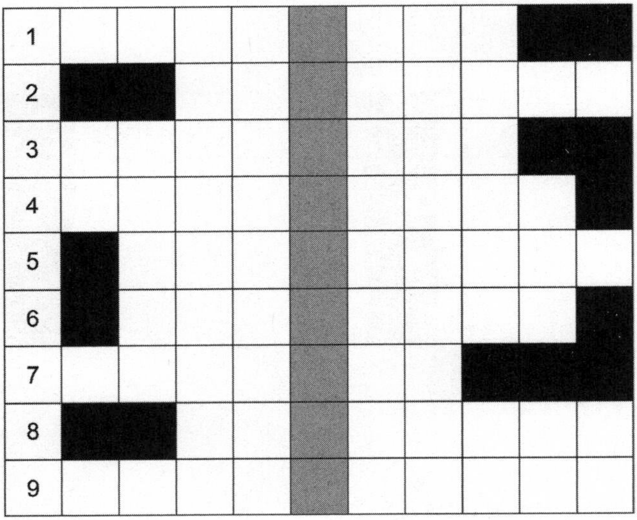

CLUES

1 TERRIBLE STACK 4,4

2 SLENDER FACIAL FEATURE 4,4

3 DOMESTICATED MONIKER 4,4

4 DARK BAG 5,4

5 DIFFICULT DEFENDER 4,5

6 EXPENSIVE ALE 4,4

7 SICK TABLET 3,4

8 HELPFUL MEMORY 4,4

9 GLOSSY BLOCK 5,5

MEMORY CIRCLE 6

Study the grid, and remember the shapes, the words and where they are positioned. Then turn the page and answer the questions.

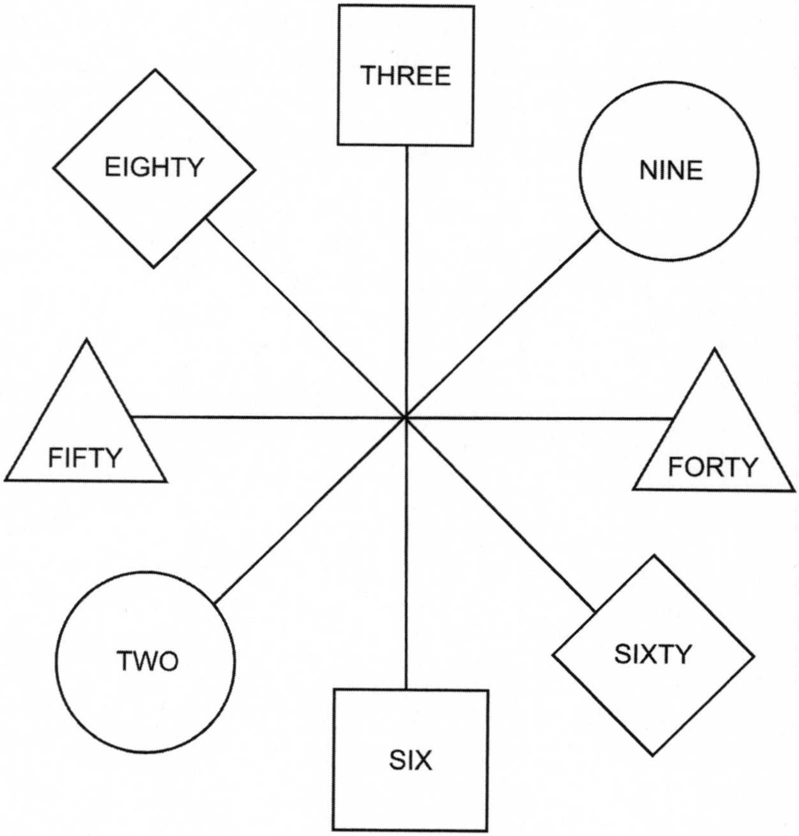

MEMORY CIRCLE 6

Questions

1. The numbers FORTY and FIFTY are in which shapes?
2. Which number is opposite THREE?
3. Which numbers are in circles?
4. Going clockwise, which shape comes after FORTY?
5. Which two numbers come between TWO and THREE?

WORD CREATION 6

Taking any two letters from a 4-letter word, use them within a new 4-letter word. Do not use the remaining two letters. For example the word after HEAT may be TAPS but *not* TAPE. Don't repeat words and avoid using proper nouns. Within 5 minutes can you create at least 45 words?

LEAP				
				45 words!

VOLVOGRAMS 6

Volvograms are words that spell another word when read backwards, for example BIN and NIB. Work out each pair of volvograms from the clues given, and then slot them into the crossword grid.

The best container (3) (3)

Boast about clothing (4) (4)

Pieces of fastening (5) (5)

Level 6

TRIANGLES 6

Each triangle contains a 3-letter, 4-letter and 5-letter word, placed in the direction of the arrows. Put the words into the correct triangles.

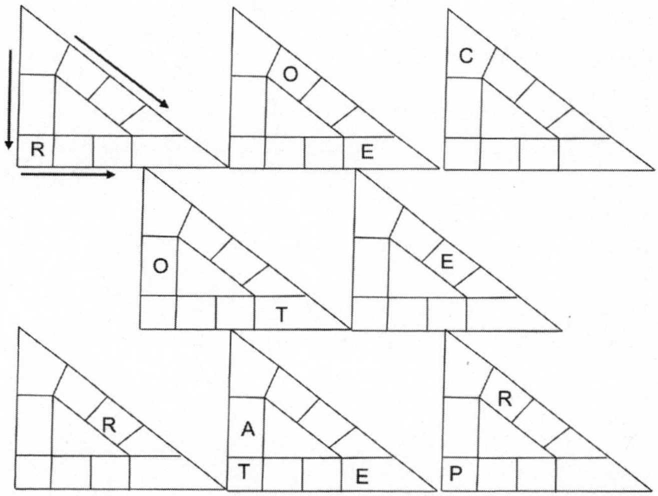

3-letter words	4-letter words	5-letter words
BAR	GAIT	BORNE
BAT	GASH	BROOM
CAP	ROAM	COACH
COG	ROLE	COMET
FOG	PUNT	FRESH
FOP	PUSH	FRONT
JAR	TALE	JORUM
JET	TERM	JOULE

NINE WORDS 6

Write one or more complete sentences using words that are 3 letters long.

Sentence

MARRIED WITH CHILDREN 6

Take 2 letters from each parent's name and combine them to form a 4-letter name of their child. The (m) or (f) indicates the gender. There may be more than one answer.

DION & VERA (m)	
SETH & DORA (f)	
VERN & DONA (m)	
ZACK & NELL (f)	

LETTER CHANGE 6

Change one letter in each of the four words so that they belong to a group of similar words. The letter to change has been underlined.

FIST	GULL	SLIM	SCALDS

PERCH	PEAT	PLUG	GRACE

HEAT	SET	SMALL	TORCH

COY	SHEER	PIE	MOAT

DUST	LAWN	DAB	RIGHT

DIAMOND WORDS 6

Find 13 words that fit the diamond grid. Avoid using the same word more than once, and words that are proper nouns.

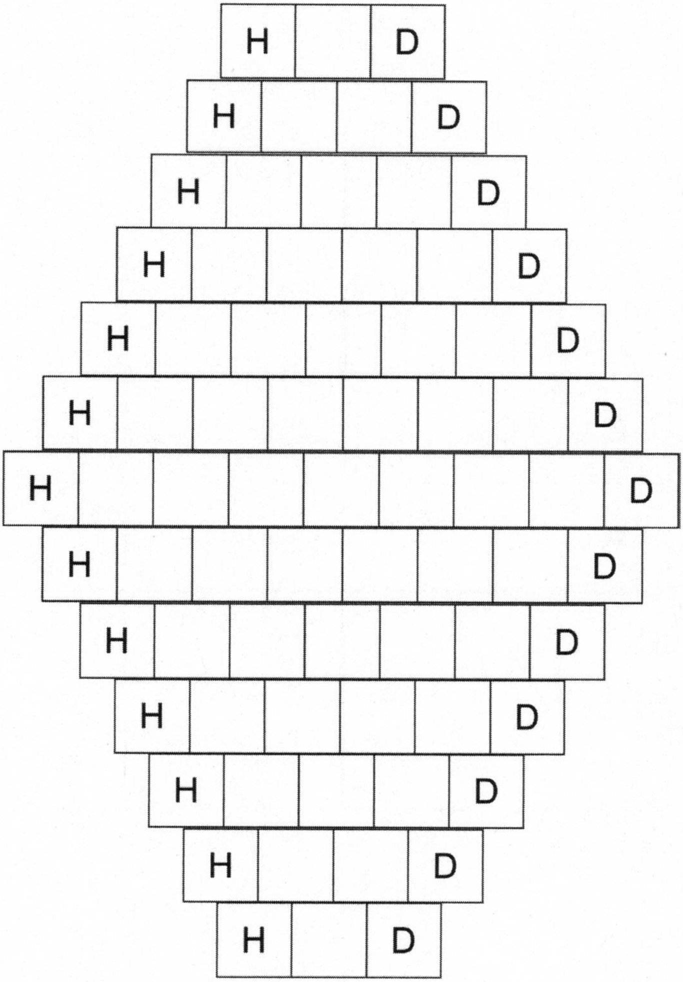

MINI WORD SUDOKU 6

Place the letters from the 6-letter word ACTION in the grid so that each column, each row, and each of the six 2×3 sub-grids contains all of the 6 letters from the word.

N	I				
		A			
C	O				I
A				O	C
			O		
				C	N

LETTER SHUFFLE 6

A saying has been placed in the grid in a continuous string, going from left to right, and reading from top to bottom. The 7 letters in the shaded squares have been rearranged.

The word lengths are: 5, 5, 8, 5, 2, 5

S	M	I	O	E
T	O	O	A	Y
T	R	M	O	R
D	O	W	C	B
U	L	D	R	E
W	O	L	S	E

Saying:

____

____

____

SPEED WORDS 6

Choose 10 words that fit the criteria given. Choose words that are not proper nouns. Use a different word for each question.

Choose a word that:		
1	Rhymes with 'VOICE'	
2	Fits into E _ E _ E _	
3	Fits into E _ E _ _ E	
4	Ends in 'GI'	
5	Is a 5 letter word ending in 'G' and does not contain the letter 'I'	
6	Has the structure: vowel vowel consonant consonant consonant	
7	Contains 2 'Z's that are not together	
8	Starts with 'Q' and has 9 letters	
9	Is an anagram of 'RAMPEP'	
10	Starts and ends with 'ING'	

Level 6

LETTER BOXES 6

Take one letter from each box to form a 5-letter word. Topic: Countries

C K C N T	E O H I O	B P R N I	E G A L E	E A O T L

CLUES 6

Solve the clues then find the letters, which are placed randomly in the grid. Cross them off, circle them, or color in the square as you find them.

CLUES

1. Shut (5)
2. Greeter of clients (12)
3. Setter of unrealistically demanding goals (13)

F	R	C	R	E
T	E	C	S	T
P	I	E	C	E
I	I	L	N	N
O	S	I	E	T
S	T	O	O	P

WORD PLUS WORD 6

Add a 3-letter word before the last letter so that it also makes a 4-letter word, for example HEM + P. Make each of the 3-letter words different. Avoid using proper nouns.

			A
			D
			E
			G
			H
			I
			K
			L
			M

MISSING ALPHABET 6

There are 9 words, each having a different letter of the alphabet missing. Work out which letter goes in each word. None of the words are proper nouns.

The letters are provided so you can cross off each one as you find it.

L_SH		HER_		FLE_
_HIP		LAD_		RA_E
UIP_		S_AY		IEW

QSUWYATVX

SQUIDS 6

Can you place the letters in the correct squares so that the grid makes 4 words that read both horizontally and vertically?

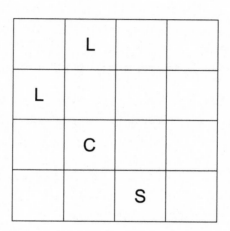

	L		
L			
	C		
		S	

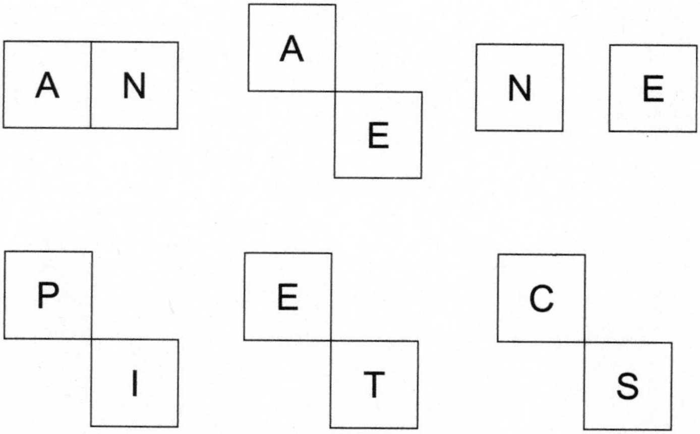

SENTENCE MAKER 6

Make up a sentence with words that fit into the structures given, where C stands for Consonant, and V stands for Vowel.

For example the sentence SHE LIKES CATS would fit into the structure CCV CVCVC CVCC. Proper nouns are allowed, and you can put punctuation anywhere in the sentence if you would like to.

C C V C ______________________________

V C ______________________________

C C ______________________________

C V C C ______________________________

C C V V C C ______________________________

WORKING IT OUT 6

Work out what these phrases have in common.

Your type? Quite pretty.

I require you to tweet.

Put your typewriter out.

Power or piety? Quit or retry? We opt out.

You were too quiet, Terry.

SYLLABLE WORDS 6

The words to find each have 3 syllables. The last syllable or section of one word forms the first syllable or section of the next, for example WONDERFUL and FULFILLING.

Starting in the centre, draw a continuous line from one word to the next. There are four words to find.

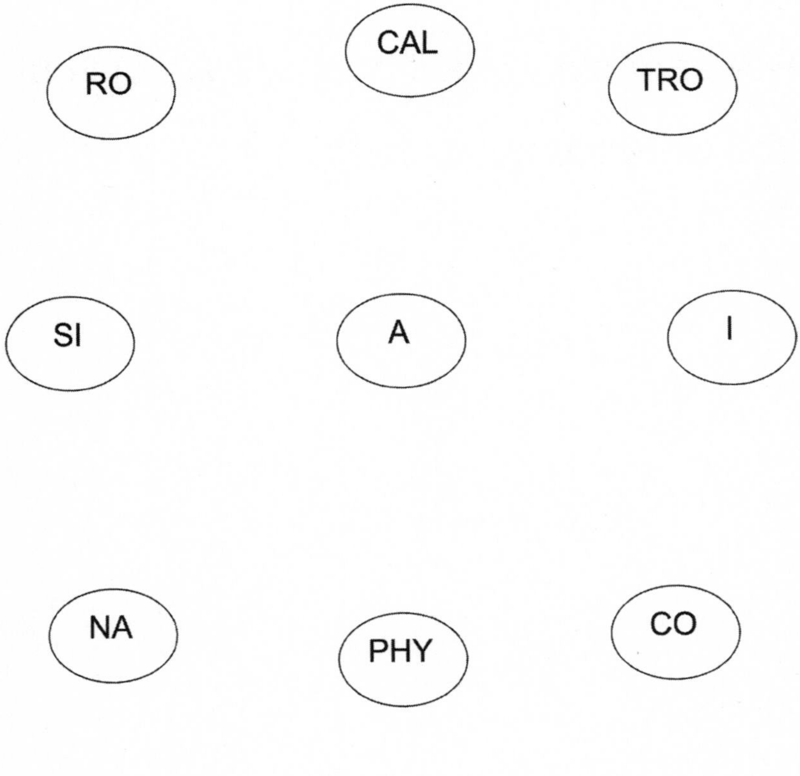

POETRY 6

Make up a traditional haiku.

Haiku are short poems originally developed by Japanese poets that often capture a feeling or image. They consist of 17 syllables, divided into three phrases: 5 syllables, 7 syllables, and 5 syllables.

Write a haiku on the topic of clouds:

MISSING LETTERS 6

Two letters are missing from each set of words. They are different letters for each set of words. What are the letters?

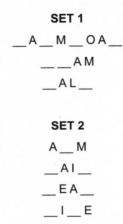

SET 1

__ A __ M __ O A __

__ __ A M

__ A L __

SET 2

A __ M

__ A I __

__ E A __

__ I __ E

WORD TRAIL 6

Find the 6 words listed in the grid starting with the circled letter. The last letter of one word forms the first letter of the next word.

Note that words can also go diagonally as well as horizontally backward or forwards, or vertically upwards or downwards.

C	A	T	H	I
T	H	C	C	T
U	H	C	N	H
H	E	(H)	U	A
T	A	H	S	R

HUNCH
HEATH
HUTCH
HATCH
HITCH
HARSH

THREE LETTERS 6

How many words can you think of that contain the three given letters in this order? They do not need to be together in the word, can occur anywhere, but need to be in this order. For example if the letters were ITE, the words could be ITEm; bITE, InnovaTE, sIsTEr, and so on.

Aim to avoid proper nouns.

You have two options here. You can spend one minute on each set of three letters, or you can choose one set of letters and spend five minutes on it.

AAR	
MOO	
MAN	
RLY	
HOE	

Level 7

ROWS AND COLUMNS 7

Fill in the column with a word that makes the rows into complete words. There are no proper nouns used. There may be more than one answer.

P	A		E
P	A		L
P	A		E
P	A		D
P	A		K

CONCENTRATION 7

Look through the passage and answer the questions.

Meaning is contextual; you obtain the meaning from the context. Some contexts are obvious, but some contexts are less obvious.

Context may be the tone of voice. Try saying "I love the works of Shakespeare" in at least a couple of different tones of voice to give it different meanings.

Context may be cultural. In some cultures averting your eyes when being spoken to is a sign of respect, in others it has a different meaning.

There may be too little context, for example in emails, where visual and vocal clues are missing.

1. How many capital letters in the passage?
2. How many two-letter words in the passage?
3. How many letter E's in the passage?

VOWEL WORDS 7

Choose words that fit the categories and include the given vowels.

The vowels can only be used once in the word, and must be in this order. They can be together or separate.

Vowels: **OE**	
One boy's name	
One girl's name	
One place name	
One creature's name	
One type of food	
One item of clothing	
A hobby or pastime	

CONTINUOUS WORDS 7

This is a list of words that have been joined together. Put the spaces in the appropriate places to work out the list of words.

ATTICCACTINATIO NCOINCAR ROTAO RTATACT-
NOONANTICCOATINTOCANNONROOTCONTACTTACO
TACITROTACORNTOOTCARTOONACTORTACTICROT
ATIONCROONACTIONTONICTRACTORRATIONTROTC
ORDCARTTORTTRACTIONROTORTORN

WORD IN WORD 7

Put the 4-letter words on the left hand side into the correct spaces to make 8-letter words.

TEEM
DEEM
EVEN
AMEN
OPEN
STEN
OVEN

U	N					E	D
L	I					E	D
E	L					T	H
S	L					L	Y
R	E					E	D
F	L					C	O
E	S					E	D

WORD RHYME 7

Find as many words as you can that rhyme with the given word. Use a timer, and take a minute for each of the five words. Note that different words rhyme in different accents, so choose words that rhyme in your accent. Decide if you want to include proper nouns or not. You can include rhyming words with different spellings, for example REED and READ.

LEEK	
HIDE	
LANK	
END	
ROUND	

HALF WORDS 7

Join two half words together to form six lots of 6-letter words.

E	R	E		C	O	C
M	O	N		M	A	S
F	A	L		C	O	A
O	O	N		C	O	M
C	O	N		C	O	H
R	S	E		C	O	T

1. ________________________
2. ________________________
3. ________________________
4. ________________________
5. ________________________
6. ________________________

X WORDS 7

Place the correct words in the rows in the grid so that both diagonals spell a five-letter word reading from top to bottom.

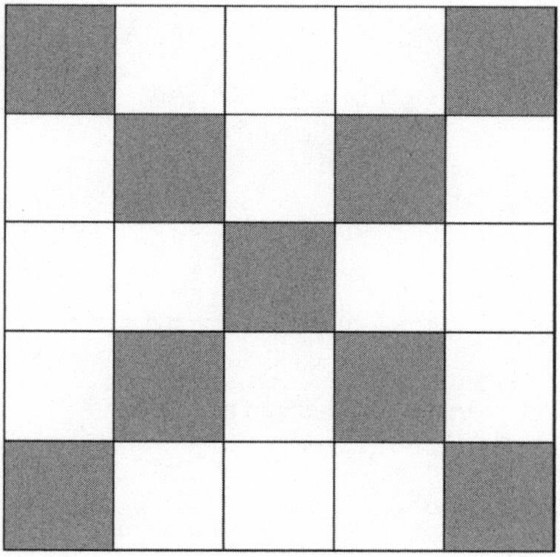

BROWN

SPINS

TENTH

MOCHA

BLESS

ALPHABET TEASERS 7

O

Find 10 words containing two O's that are not together

R

Find 10 words that start and end in R

Z

Find 10 words containing ZZ that are not plurals

ANAGRAM GRID 7

Solve the anagrams and place them into the correct spaces in the grid.
Two letters have been placed for you.

STEAK
LEAST
KLEAN
KEANS

I LIKE ... 7

All the items *'I like*' have a connection that the items *'I don't like'* do not have. Can you work out the connection?

I LIKE ...	... BUT I DON'T LIKE
Hannah	Leanne
kayak	canoe
madam	sir
minim	crotchet
racecar	motor
stats	numbers
radar	sonar
level	straight

WORD FLOW 7

Think of four 6-letter words that start with the letters on the left and end with the letter in the middle. Then think of four 6-letter words that start with the letter in the middle and end with the letters on the right. Avoid using proper nouns.

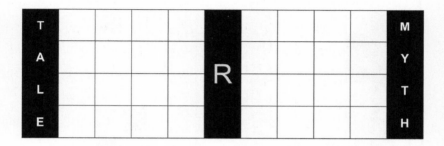

<table>
<tr><td>T</td><td></td><td></td><td></td><td></td><td rowspan="4">R</td><td></td><td></td><td></td><td></td><td>M</td></tr>
<tr><td>A</td><td></td><td></td><td></td><td></td><td></td><td></td><td></td><td></td><td>Y</td></tr>
<tr><td>L</td><td></td><td></td><td></td><td></td><td></td><td></td><td></td><td></td><td>T</td></tr>
<tr><td>E</td><td></td><td></td><td></td><td></td><td></td><td></td><td></td><td></td><td>H</td></tr>
</table>

RHYME TIME 7

Each row in the grid contains two words that rhyme—an adjective and a noun.

Solve the clues then slot the words into the grid so that the gray column also contains two rhyming words.

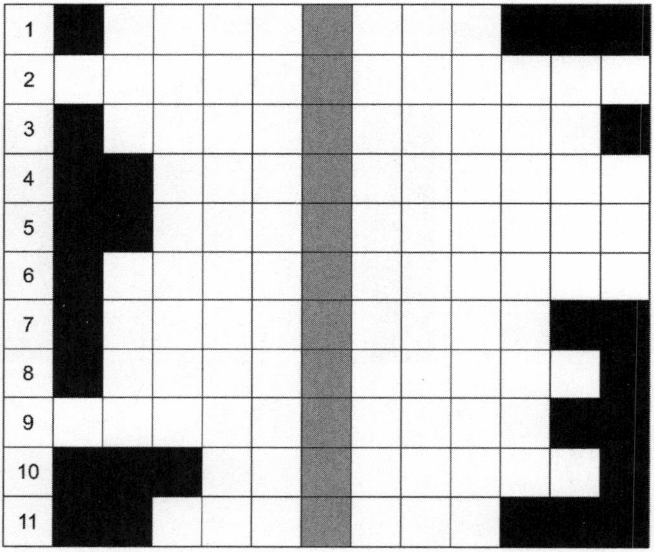

CLUES

1 OFFENSIVE DINNER 4,4

2 IMPROVED CORRESPONDENCE 6,6

3 UPTIGHT BARRIER 5,5

4 AMUSING RABBIT 5,5

5 LOOSE SHED 5,5

6 GLEAMING ILLUMINATION 6,5

7 HUGE EXPLOSION 4,5

8 COURAGEOUS RESTING PLACE 5,5

9 MILKY EVENING 5,5

10 FILIGREE COMPETITION 4,4

11 ELEVATED HEAVENS 4,3

Level 7

MEMORY CIRCLE 7

Study the grid, and remember the shapes, the words and where they are positioned. Then turn the page and answer the questions.

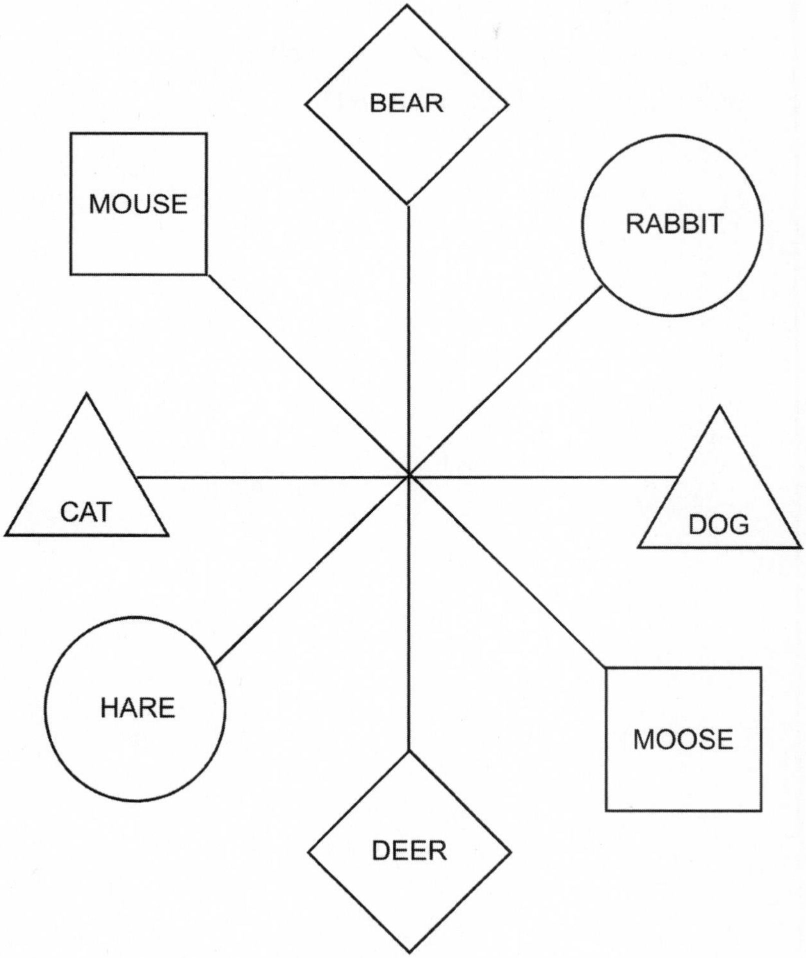

MEMORY CIRCLE 7

Questions

1. Which word is in the top diamond shape?
2. Which words are in circles?
3. Which word is opposite MOOSE?
4. Which word and shape are at the bottom?
5. Which words are in the triangles?

WORD CREATION 7

Taking the first letter of a word, use it as the last letter of a new word of any length. For example the word after HEAL may be PATCH. Don't repeat words and avoid using proper nouns. Within 5 minutes can you create at least 40 words?

PAIL				
				40 words!

VOLVOGRAMS 7

Volvograms are words that spell another word when read backwards, for example BIN and NIB. Work out each pair of volvograms from the clues given, and then slot them into the crossword grid.

Spoil a sheep (3) (3)		
Border on an instrument (4) (4)		
Dried stalks, grow on skin (5) (5)		

TRIANGLES 7

Each triangle contains a 3-letter, 4-letter and 5-letter word, placed in the direction of the arrows. Put the words into the correct triangles.

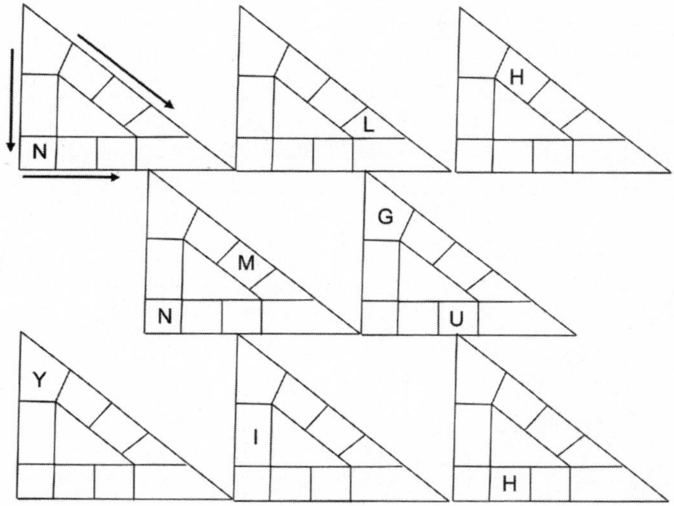

3-letter words	4-letter words	5-letter words
BIG	GLUE	BRAIN
BIN	GRIN	BRINE
GAS	NINE	GOING
GUT	NOUN	GRAND
WIG	SLID	WHERE
WIN	SNUG	WOMEN
YES	THUD	YIELD
YET	TWIG	YOUNG

NINE WORDS 7

Write one or more complete sentences using words of any length that start with a vowel.

Sentence

MARRIED WITH CHILDREN 7

Take 2 letters from each parent's name and combine them to form a 4-letter name of their child. The (m) or (f) indicates the gender. There may be more than one answer.

PETE & LOLA (f)	
RICH & OPAL (m)	
RICK & KATH (f)	
HANS & ROMY (m)	

LETTER CHANGE 7

Change one letter in each of the four words so that they belong to a group of similar words. The letter to change has been underlined.

TAR	EVE	NOSH	MONTH

PEG	KNEW	FORT	SKIN

ORE	TOO	THREW	HOUR

PUP	SLATE	WISH	BOIL

PORE	LIMB	BEER	TEAL

Level 7

DIAMOND WORDS 7

Find 13 words that fit the diamond grid. Avoid using the same word more than once, and words that are proper nouns.

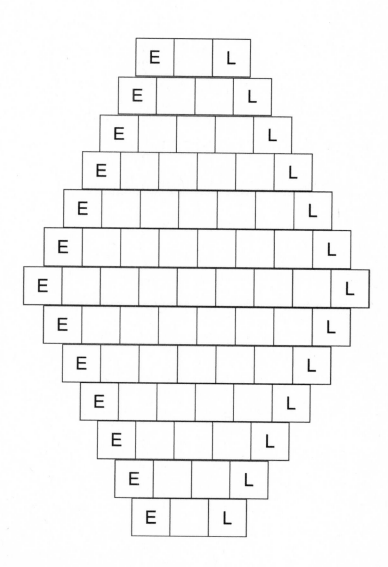

E		L						
E			L					
E				L				
E					L			
E						L		
E							L	
E								L
E							L	
E						L		
E					L			
E				L				
E			L					
E		L						

MINI WORD SUDOKU 7

Place the letters from the 6-letter word **PRAXIS** in the grid so that each column, each row, and each of the six 2×3 sub-grids contains all of the 6 letters from the word.

S				A	
		R		S	
			X		
		A			
	I		A		
	A				P

LETTER SHUFFLE 7

A saying has been placed in the grid in a continuous string, going from left to right, and reading from top to bottom. The 7 letters in the shaded squares have been rearranged.

The word lengths are: 7, 2, 2, 5, 5, 3, 3, 3

G	R	O	T	I
N	G	O	P	I
S	W	R	E	A
U	U	N	T	U
L	Y	O	G	G
E	T	I	L	D

Saying:

____

____

____

SPEED WORDS 7

Choose 10 words that fit the criteria given. Choose words that are not proper nouns. Use a different word for each question.

Choose a word that:		
1	Has 7 letters and starts and ends with 'L'	
2	Has 4 syllables and ends in 'A'	
3	Starts with 'INC' and has 5 syllables	
4	Fits into U _ _ _ _ Y	
5	Has 2 lots of double letters that are the same	
6	Has 2 lots of double letters that are different	
7	Has 6 letters and starts with a double letter	
8	Contains the combination of letters 'ARR' in the body of the word	
9	Starts with 'I' and ends with 'A'	
10	Is an anagram of 'COOLTEACH'	

Level 7

LETTER BOXES 7

Take one letter from each box to form a 5-letter word. Topic: Food

P B S S C	T A A U U	C E S S R	H A R T O	N I Y A K

CLUES 7

Solve the clues then find the letters, which are placed randomly in the grid. Cross them off, circle them, or color in the square as you find them.

CLUES

1. Musical instrument (5)
2. Tutor (7)
3. Largest animal (4,5)
4. Maker of wooden objects (9)

I	E	E	T	E
N	E	U	P	W
C	H	A	N	T
R	L	R	A	A
R	B	E	O	L
P	E	A	C	H

WORD PLUS WORD 7

Add a 3-letter word before the last letter so that it also makes a 4-letter word, for example HEM + P. Make each of the 3-letter words different. Avoid using plurals and proper nouns.

			N
			O
			P
			R
			S
			T
			Y
			B
			F

MISSING ALPHABET 7

There are 9 words, each having a different letter of the alphabet missing. Work out which letter goes in each word. None of the words are proper nouns.

The letters are provided so you can cross off each one as you find it.

CA_E		B_TTER		COA_
_EAL		CIVI_		_RINGE
TW_N		SIL_Y		CO_L

ZCFILORUX

SQUIDS 7

Can you place the letters in the correct squares so that the grid makes 5 words that read both horizontally and vertically?

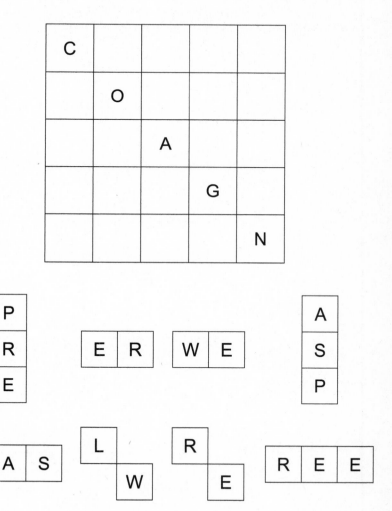

C				
	O			
		A		
			G	
				N

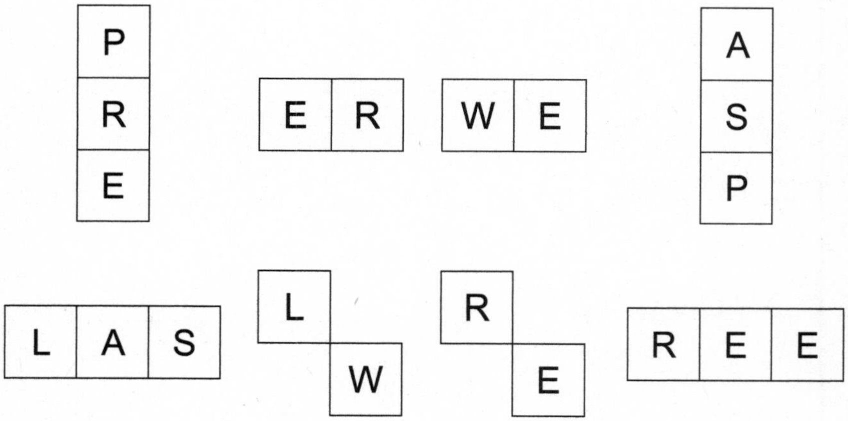

SENTENCE MAKER 7

Make up a sentence with words that fit into the structures given, where C stands for Consonant, and V stands for Vowel.

For example the sentence SHE LIKES CATS would fit into the structure CCV CVCVC CVCC. Proper nouns are allowed, and you can put punctuation anywhere in the sentence if you would like to.

V ____________________

C V C V ____________________

C V ____________________

C V V C ____________________

V C ____________________

C C V C C C ____________________

C C V C V C C C ____________________

WORKING IT OUT 7

Work out what these phrases have in common.

John hugs lost lamb.

Will Katy want pork?

Many find cars dull.

Sand felt very warm.

Work hard till dusk.

SYLLABLE WORDS 7

The words to find each have 3 syllables. The last syllable or section of one word forms the first syllable or section of the next, for example WONDERFUL and FULFILLING.

Starting in the centre, draw a continuous line from one word to the next. There are four words to find.

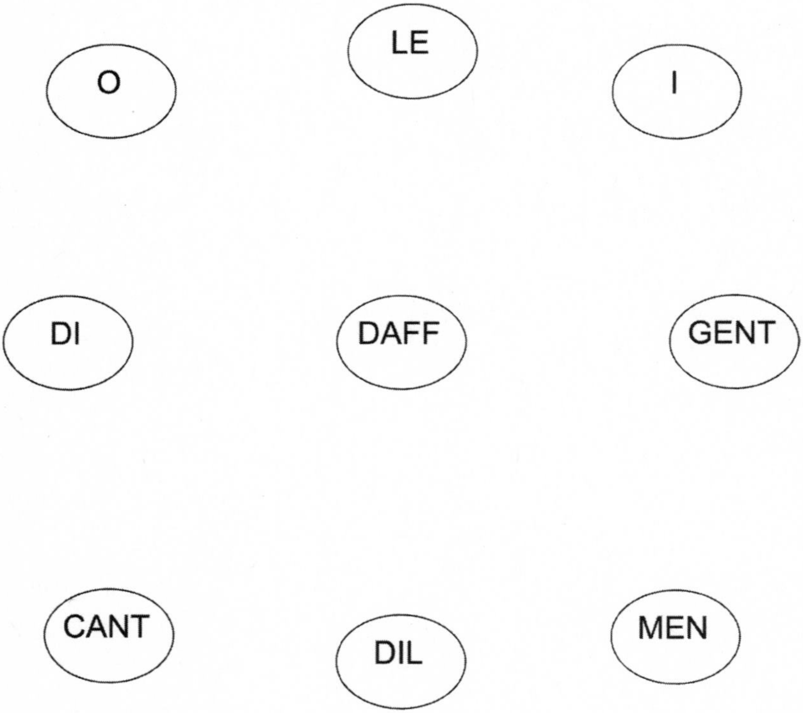

POETRY 7

Make up a limerick.

A limerick is a humorous poem consisting of a stanza of five lines, where the first, second and fifth lines rhyme with each other, and the third and fourth lines also rhyme with each other. Often the first line introduces a person or a location which is placed at the end to establish the rhyme scheme for the second and fifth lines.

The speech stress is shown in the example:

There *once* was a *young* man called *Phil*

Who *lived* at the *top* of a *hill*

He *wanted* to *fly*

High *up* in the *sky*

So *sprouted* some *wings* and a *bill*.

The first line is given:

I used to go cycling in Spain

____

____

____

____

MISSING LETTERS 7

Two letters are missing from each set of words. They are different letters for each set of words. What are the letters?

SET 1

_ _ E W

A _ _ E

I T _ _

S U _ _

SET 2

_ _ E W

A _ _ E

_ I _ E

_ U L _

WORD TRAIL 7

Find the 6 words listed in the grid starting with the circled letter. The last letter of one word forms the first letter of the next word.

Note that words can also go diagonally as well as horizontally backward or forwards, or vertically upwards or downwards.

D	E	I	V	E
I	C	(D)	D	R
N	I	D	A	E
D	E	D	D	E
I	U	R	R	I

DIVED
DREAD
DICED
DINED
DRIED
DRUID

THREE LETTERS 7

How many words can you think of that contain the three given letters in this order? They do not need to be together in the word, can occur anywhere, but need to be in this order. For example if the letters were ITE, the words could be ITEm; bITE, InnovaTE, sIsTEr, and so on.

Aim to avoid proper nouns.

You have two options here. You can spend one minute on each set of three letters, or you can choose one set of letters and spend five minutes on it.

D I N	
L T E	
T H N	
I I N	
C K E	

Level 8

ROWS AND COLUMNS 8

Fill in the column with a word that makes the rows into complete words. There are no proper nouns used. There may be more than one answer.

S		O	P
S		O	W
S		L	K
S		A	P
S		I	N

CONTINUOUS WORDS 8

This is a list of words that have been joined together. Put the spaces in the appropriate places to work out the list of words.

CANECHAPARCHERCAREERCHEAPNEARPARCH-
HENCECRANEPANEPEACEPACEACHECAREHEAPPE
ACHPEERCHEERAREACARPNAPEPEARACREPERCH
CHEEPHERERACERANCHARCHRAREREAPARENAHE
ARREARREACH

WORD IN WORD 8

Put the 4-letter words on the left hand side into the correct spaces to make 8-letter words.

<table>
<tr><td rowspan="7">OVEN
EVER
EWER
OVER
OMEN
EVEN
AMEN</td><td>C</td><td></td><td></td><td></td><td></td><td>A</td><td>G</td><td>E</td></tr>
<tr><td>C</td><td></td><td></td><td></td><td></td><td>A</td><td>N</td><td>T</td></tr>
<tr><td>S</td><td></td><td></td><td></td><td></td><td>T</td><td>H</td><td>S</td></tr>
<tr><td>L</td><td></td><td></td><td></td><td></td><td>T</td><td>E</td><td>D</td></tr>
<tr><td>S</td><td></td><td></td><td></td><td></td><td>A</td><td>G</td><td>E</td></tr>
<tr><td>M</td><td></td><td></td><td></td><td></td><td>T</td><td>U</td><td>M</td></tr>
<tr><td>S</td><td></td><td></td><td></td><td></td><td>I</td><td>T</td><td>Y</td></tr>
</table>

WORD RHYME 8

Find as many words as you can that rhyme with the given word. Use a timer, and take a minute for each of the five words. Note that different words rhyme in different accents, so choose words that rhyme in your accent. Decide if you want to include proper nouns or not. You can include rhyming words with different spellings, for example REED and READ.

ALE	
CAT	
IN	
BILL	
CAKE	

HALF WORDS 8

Join two half words together to form seven lots of 6-letter words.

T A L	H A L
L O P	L A P
L A W	E N T
O U T	O N S
L E T	P O T
L O W	W A L
T O P	H O L

1. ____________________
2. ____________________
3. ____________________
4. ____________________
5. ____________________
6. ____________________
7. ____________________

X WORDS 8

Place the correct words in the rows in the grid so that both diagonals spell a five-letter word reading from top to bottom.

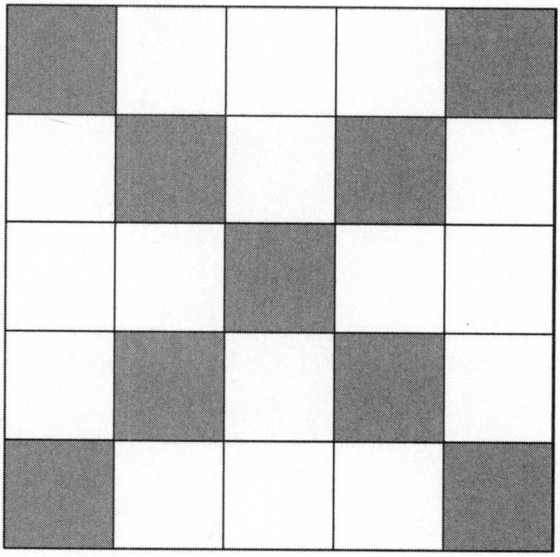

GLORY

POINT

NOISE

LIONS

FRAME

ALPHABET TEASERS 8

H

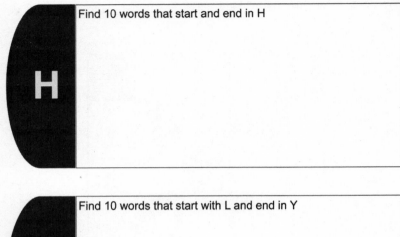

Find 10 words that start and end in H

L

Find 10 words that start with L and end in Y

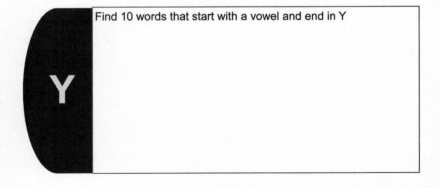

Y

Find 10 words that start with a vowel and end in Y

Level 8

ANAGRAM GRID 8

Solve the anagrams and place them into the correct spaces in the grid. Two letters have been placed for you.

ACERD

ACERT

ACERT

ACERT

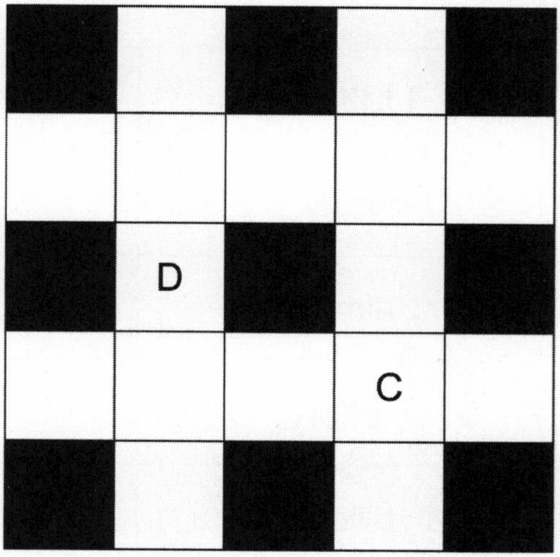

I LIKE ... 8

All the items *'I like'* have a connection that the items *'I don't like'* do not have. Can you work out the connection?

I LIKE ...	... BUT I DON'T LIKE
forty	fifty
almost	nearly
effort	attempt
billowy	cloudy
abhor	detest
chintz	calico
abet	help
ghost	spirit

WORD FLOW 8

Think of four 6-letter words that start with the letters on the left and end with the letter in the middle. Then think of four 6-letter words that start with the letter in the middle and end with the letters on the right. Avoid using proper nouns.

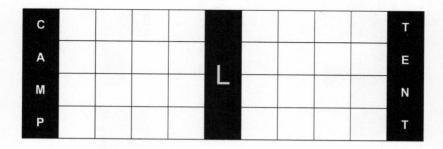

<table>
<tr><td>C</td><td></td><td></td><td></td><td></td><td rowspan="4">L</td><td></td><td></td><td></td><td></td><td>T</td></tr>
<tr><td>A</td><td></td><td></td><td></td><td></td><td></td><td></td><td></td><td></td><td>E</td></tr>
<tr><td>M</td><td></td><td></td><td></td><td></td><td></td><td></td><td></td><td></td><td>N</td></tr>
<tr><td>P</td><td></td><td></td><td></td><td></td><td></td><td></td><td></td><td></td><td>T</td></tr>
</table>

RHYME TIME 8

Each row in the grid contains two words that rhyme—an adjective and a noun.

Solve the clues then slot the words into the grid so that the gray column also contains two rhyming words.

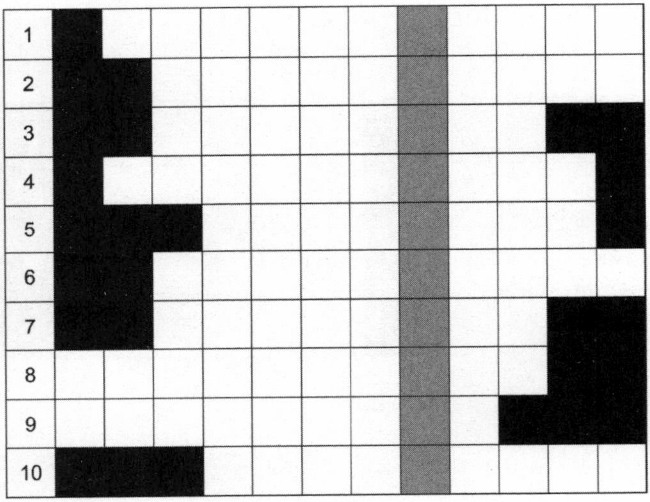

CLUES

1 RECTANGULAR STEP 6,5

2 CIRCULAR DOG 5,5

3 CHILLY WATER 4,4

4 SHORT SADNESS 5,5

5 CROOKED SHELTER 4,4

6 SATISFIED MASS OF WATER DROPS 5,5

7 BRAVE METAL 4,4

8 INEBRIATED MAMMAL 5,5

9 UNINTERESTED NOBLEMAN 5,4

10 TIDY PLEASURE 4,5

MEMORY CIRCLE 8

Study the grid, and remember the shapes, the words and where they are positioned. Then turn the page and answer the questions.

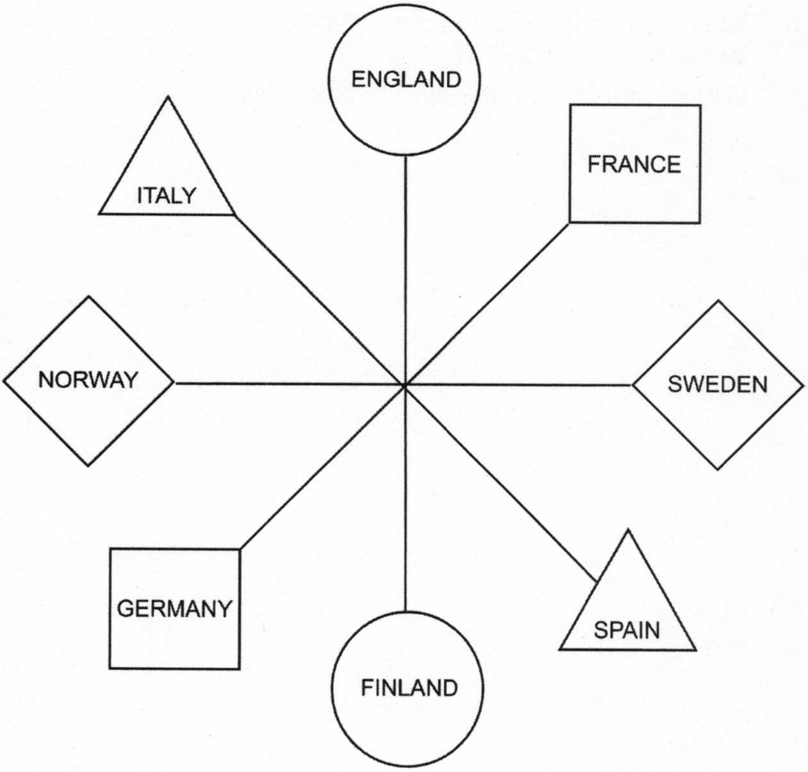

MEMORY CIRCLE 8

Questions

1. Which countries start with a vowel?
2. Which countries are in squares?
3. Which country is opposite NORWAY?
4. Which 2 countries come after SWEDEN, going in a clockwise direction?
5. Which country is in the North West position?

WORD CREATION 8

Using a **4-letter** word starting with '**S**' create another 4-letter word starting with 'S' that does **not** include the last letter of the previous word. For example the word after SEAL may be STAY, but could not be SLAY. Don't repeat words and avoid using proper nouns. Within 5 minutes can you create at least 45 words?

SOUP				
				45 words!

VOLVOGRAMS 8

Volvograms are words that spell another word when read backwards, for example BIN and NIB. Work out each pair of volvograms from the clues given, and then slot them into the crossword grid.

Talented Italian island (4) (4)

Prove potato is false (5) (5)

Recompense a storage compartment (6) (6)

TRIANGLES 8

Each triangle contains a 3-letter, 4-letter and 5-letter word, placed in the direction of the arrows. Put the words into the correct triangles.

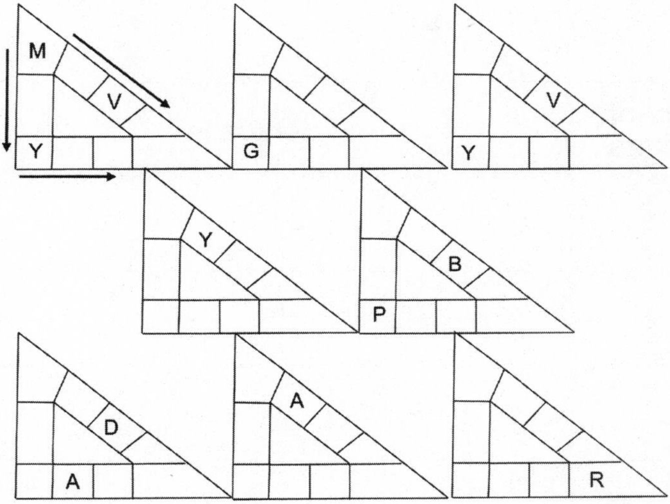

3-letter words	4-letter words	5-letter words
MAN	GAIN	MAVEN
MAP	GATE	MEDAL
MAY	NAIL	MOUSE
MUG	NEAR	MOVER
NAN	PAIN	NADIR
NAP	PATE	NOBLE
NAY	YEAR	NOVEL
NOG	YELL	NYLON

NINE WORDS 8

Write one or more complete sentences using words that start with a vowel and contain 1 through to 9 letters.

No. of letters	Sentence
1	
2	
3	
4	
5	
6	
7	
8	
9	

MARRIED WITH CHILDREN 8

Take 2 letters from each parent's name and combine them to form a 4-letter name of their child. The (m) or (f) indicates the gender. There may be more than one answer.

MICK & KARA (m)	
TONY & KIRA (f)	
LEON & RUTH (m)	
ANDY & AMIE (f)	

LETTER CHANGE 8

Change one letter in each of the four words so that they belong to a group of similar words. The letter to change has been underlined.

BENCH	SHORT	SAID	SPA

HIND	PAIL	THUMP	PALL

SLIP	BEAT	LARGE	BERRY

SEVER	LIGHT	WINE	TEA

KINE	PRANCE	EARS	FORD

DIAMOND WORDS 8

Find 13 words that fit the diamond grid. Avoid using the same word more than once, and words that are proper nouns.

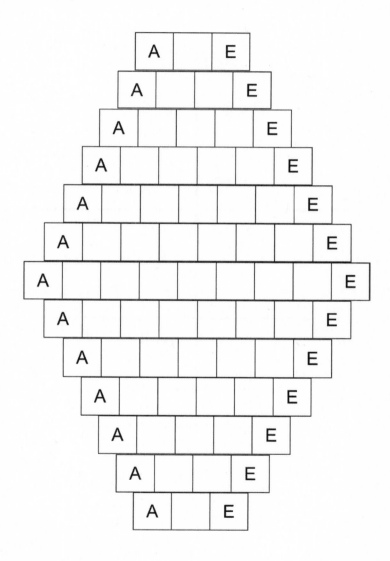

A		E						
A			E					
A				E				
A					E			
A						E		
A							E	
A								E
A							E	
A						E		
A					E			
A				E				
A			E					
A		E						

MINI WORD SUDOKU 8

Place the letters from the 6-letter word CLAUSE in the grid so that each column, each row, and each of the six 2×3 sub-grids contains all of the 6 letters from the word.

L		E		A	
A				C	
	C				U
	A		C		S

Level 8

LETTER SHUFFLE 8

A saying has been placed in the grid in a continuous string, going from left to right, and reading from top to bottom. The 8 letters in the shaded squares have been rearranged.

The word lengths are: 1, 8, 4, 5, 1, 6, 2, 4, 4

A	B	A	C	A
N	C	I	D	D
I	H	T	M	E
E	N	S	A	E
O	O	K	L	E
I	N	A	A	C
H	E	A	N	D

Saying:

____

____

____

SPEED WORDS 8

Choose 10 words that fit the criteria given. Choose words that are not proper nouns. Use a different word for each question.

Choose a word that:		
1	Has 5 letters and ends with 'X'	
2	Has the structure: consonant vowel vowel vowel	
3	Starts with 'J' and ends with 'W' and has more than 3 letters	
4	Has 11 letters and starts with 'W'	
5	Has 10 letters and ends with 'Y'	
6	Contains 3 'S's	
7	Has 3 syllables and ends in 'GY'	
8	Has 7 letters with 'X' in the middle	
9	Is an anagram of 'DESERTPIN'	
10	Rhymes with 'DRIBBLE'	

LETTER BOXES 8

Take one letter from each box to form a 5-letter word. Topic: Emotions

P G W S S	C O R H U	I I A O R	M R L R D	Y E E T N

CLUES 8

Solve the clues then find the letters, which are placed randomly in the grid. Cross them off, circle them, or color in the square as you find them.

CLUES

1. Planet (4)
2. Month (5)
3. Continent (6)
4. Season (6)
5. Rainbow color (6)
6. Arctic animal (5,4)

A	A	I	A	A	I
B	V	I	O	E	M
S	A	M	P	L	E
R	U	L	F	C	E
S	R	R	R	R	M
P	O	R	T	A	L

WORD PLUS WORD 8

Add a 3-letter word before the last letter so that it also makes a 4-letter word, for example HEM + P. Make each of the 3-letter words different. Avoid using proper nouns.

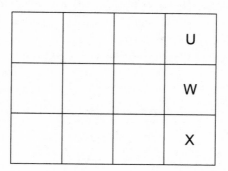

			U
			W
			X

Add a 4-letter word before the last letter so that it also makes a 5-letter word, for example STAR + E. Make each of the 4-letter words different. Avoid using plurals and proper nouns.

				B
				D
				E
				F
				G
				H

MISSING ALPHABET 8

There are 10 words, each having a different letter of the alphabet missing. Work out which letter goes in each word. None of the words are proper nouns.

The letters are provided so you can cross off each one as you find it.

PIN_	_OON	FAT_ER
PRI_E	S_EAK	PLA_UE
PO_D	LI_E	HORNE_
	_EEDY	

B E H K N Q T W Z D

SQUIDS 8

Can you place the letters in the correct squares so that the grid makes 5 words that read both horizontally and vertically?

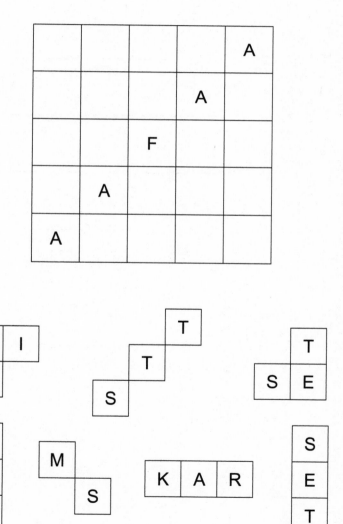

				A
			A	
		F		
	A			
A				

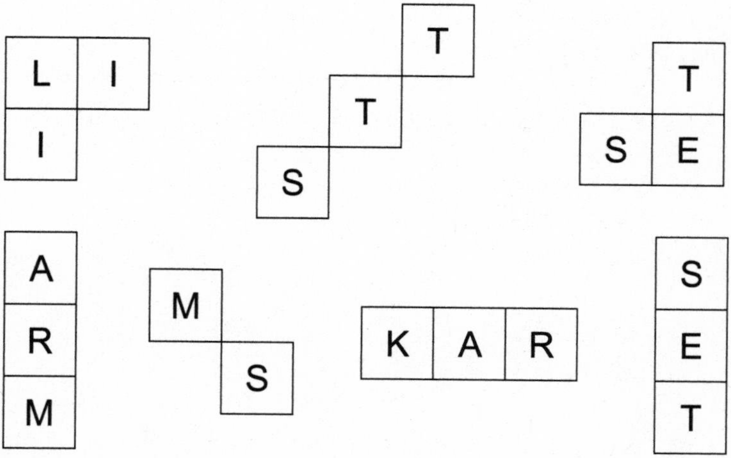

SENTENCE MAKER 8

Make up a sentence with words that fit into the structures given, where C stands for Consonant, and V stands for Vowel.

For example the sentence SHE LIKES CATS would fit into the structure CCV CVCVC CVCC. Proper nouns are allowed, and you can put punctuation anywhere in the sentence if you would like to.

C C ______________________________

C V C ______________________________

V C ______________________________

V ______________________________

C V V C ______________________________

C V V C C V C ______________________________

WORKING IT OUT 8

Work out what these phrases have in common.

You are my best friend.

Jordan orders seven stylish laptops.

Helena constantly recruited competent employees.

Theodora's education prohibited historical exploration.

Sophisticated Yugoslavians accumulated enthusiastic Argentinians.

SYLLABLE WORDS 8

The words to find each have 3 syllables. The last syllable or section of one word forms the first syllable or section of the next, for example WONDERFUL and FULFILLING.

Starting in the centre, draw a continuous line from one word to the next. There are five words to find.

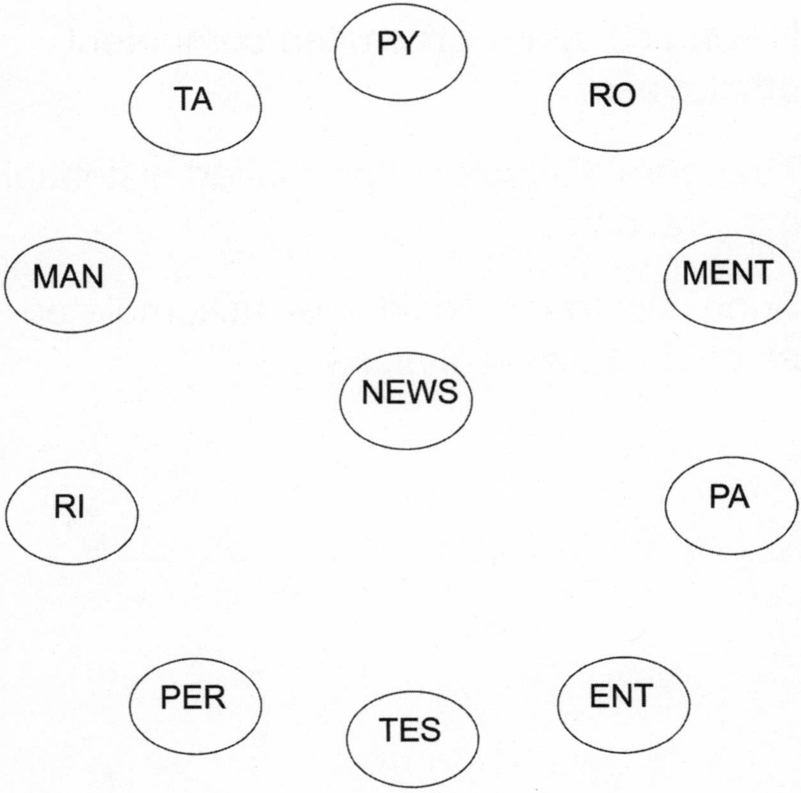

POETRY 8

Make up a limerick.

A limerick is a humorous poem consisting of a stanza of five lines, where the first, second and fifth lines rhyme with each other, and the third and fourth lines also rhyme with each other. Often the first line introduces a person or a location, which is placed at the end to establish the rhyme scheme for the second and fifth lines.

The first line is given:

A cuddly young puppy called Spot

____

____

____

____

MISSING LETTERS 8

Two letters are missing from each set of words. They are different letters for each set of words. What are the letters?

SET 1

__ __ B L E

A __ __ R

__ R __ I N

S U __ __ R

SET 2

__ __ B L E

A __ __ R

A __ R __ I D

__ __ C E

Level 8

WORD TRAIL 8

Find the 6 words listed in the grid starting with the circled letter. The last letter of one word forms the first letter of the next word.

Note that words can also go diagonally as well as horizontally backward or forwards, or vertically upwards or downwards.

A	D	A	V	E
G	E	E	S	(E)
L	L	T	A	L
E	A	I	R	U
T	E	L	D	E

ELUDE
ERASE
EVADE
EAGLE
ELATE
ELITE

THREE LETTERS 8

How many words can you think of that contain the three given letters in this order? They do not need to be together in the word, can occur anywhere, but need to be in this order. For example if the letters were ITE, the words could be ITEm; bITE, InnovaTE, sIsTEr, and so on.

Aim to avoid proper nouns.

You have two options here. You can spend one minute on each set of three letters, or you can choose one set of letters and spend five minutes on it.

B B E	
F F Y	
E G H	
L M N	
U S T	

Level 9

ROWS AND COLUMNS 9

Fill in the column with a word that makes the rows into complete words. There are no proper nouns used. There may be more than one answer.

M	A		S
D	A		E
W	I		E
L	E		N
C	A		E

CONCENTRATION 9

Put a circle around the words where the letters are in alphabetical order

JUG	ELK	SKY	VIE
HIP	ZIP	GET	ART
LOT	OLD	ANT	INK
AIR	KEY	COW	POT
WHY	DIN	MET	DEW
FAR	RAY	YOU	NOT
STY	KIT	BAT	URN
BIT	WAX	CRY	EAR
CAP	GIN	JAR	LOP
NUT	USE	TWO	FIR
PEW	MOP	RUT	ZEN
DOT	IRE	YET	HOT
TOY	OUT	BOW	VEX

VOWEL WORDS 9

Choose words that fit the categories and include the given vowels.

The vowels can only be used once in the word, and must be in this order. They can be together or separate.

Vowels: **EA**	
Two boys' names	
Two girls' names	
Two place name	
Two creatures' names	
Two types of food	
Two colors	
A hobby or pastime	

CONTINUOUS WORDS 9

This is a list of words that have been joined together. Put the spaces in the appropriate places to work out the list of words.

HOTTERLOREHEALERWEARHOLEMOATHORROR-
MOLEHOMEOATHHOWLWHOLEOTHERLOATHEHOTEL
MOTHERLOWERHERORATHERROLEWROTEMOTHHO
LLERTHREWROTETHERETHROATRAREHOLLOWWEA
LTHTOREREALWHEREMOREWORTHTOWERWORETO
WELWRATHTHROW

WORD IN WORD 9

Put the 4-letter words on the left hand side into the correct spaces to make 8-letter words.

<table>
<tr><td rowspan="8">HILL
WILL
PILL
KILL
TALL
CALL
WALL</td><td>S</td><td></td><td></td><td></td><td></td><td>A</td><td>G</td><td>E</td></tr>
<tr><td>S</td><td></td><td></td><td></td><td></td><td>I</td><td>O</td><td>N</td></tr>
<tr><td>S</td><td></td><td></td><td></td><td></td><td>O</td><td>P</td><td>S</td></tr>
<tr><td>S</td><td></td><td></td><td></td><td></td><td>F</td><td>U</td><td>L</td></tr>
<tr><td>C</td><td></td><td></td><td></td><td></td><td>I</td><td>N</td><td>G</td></tr>
<tr><td>S</td><td></td><td></td><td></td><td></td><td>O</td><td>W</td><td>S</td></tr>
<tr><td>S</td><td></td><td></td><td></td><td></td><td>I</td><td>N</td><td>G</td></tr>
<tr><td>S</td><td></td><td></td><td></td><td></td><td>O</td><td>T</td><td>S</td></tr>
</table>

WORD RHYME 9

Find as many words as you can that rhyme with the given word. Use a timer, and take a minute for each of the five words. Note that different words rhyme in different accents, so choose words that rhyme in your accent. Decide if you want to include proper nouns or not. You can include rhyming words with different spellings, for example REED and READ.

LANE	
LOCK	
MAN	
HOOT	
IT	

HALF WORDS 9

Join two half words together to form seven lots of 6-letter words.

H E S	H E L
T L E	T E L
R I C	C R I
H O S	H U S
S T Y	S H Y
B U S	S P Y
S L U	L U S

1. ______________________
2. ______________________
3. ______________________
4. ______________________
5. ______________________
6. ______________________
7. ______________________

X WORDS 9

Place the correct words in the rows in the grid so that both diagonals spell a five-letter word reading from top to bottom.

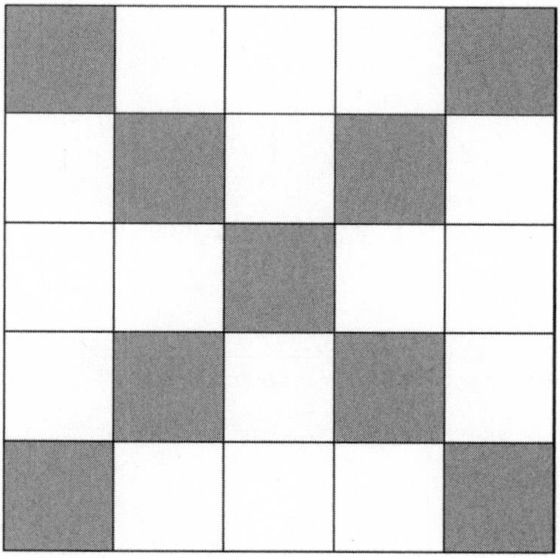

SEVEN

SCORE

HERON

STAMP

LEAST

ALPHABET TEASERS 4

C

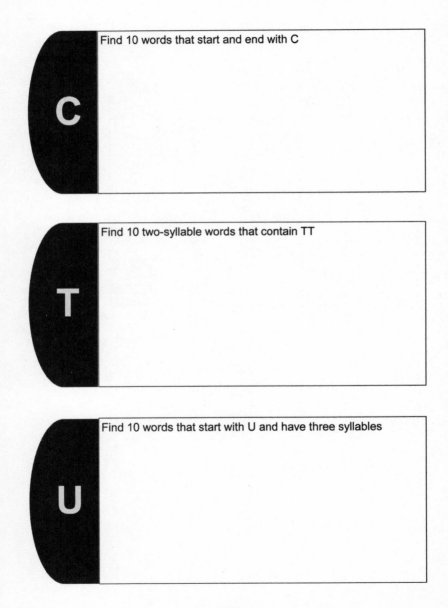

Find 10 words that start and end with C

T

Find 10 two-syllable words that contain TT

U

Find 10 words that start with U and have three syllables

ANAGRAM GRID 9

Solve the anagrams and place them into the correct spaces in the grid.
One letter has been placed for you.

SLACS
IVECO
VEILA
EVISE
CLIIV
IGLEE

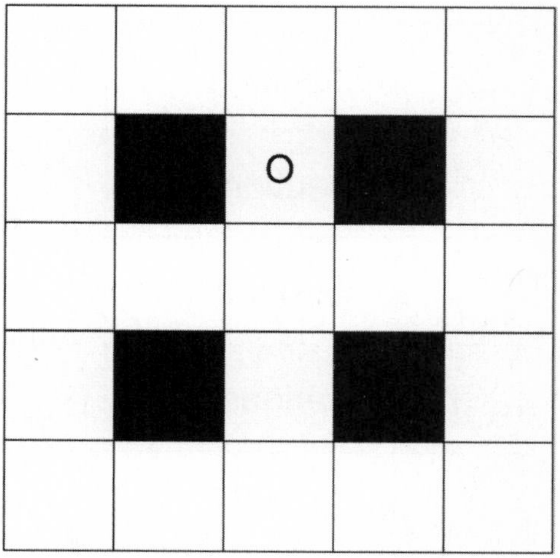

I LIKE ... 9

All the items *'I like'* have a connection that the items *'I don't like'* do not have. Can you work out the connection?

I LIKE ...	... BUT I DON'T LIKE
education	schooling
precaution	prevention
tambourine	cymbal
precarious	dangerous
regulation	official
authorize	permission
facetious	annoying
sequoia	redwood

WORD FLOW 9

Think of four 6-letter words that start with the letters on the left and end with the letter in the middle. Then think of four 6-letter words that start with the letter in the middle and end with the letters on the right. Avoid using proper nouns.

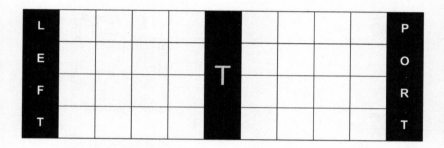

L					T					P
E					T					O
F					T					R
T					T					T

RHYME TIME 9

Each row in the grid contains two words that rhyme—an adjective and a noun.

Solve the clues then slot the words into the grid so that the gray column also contains two rhyming words.

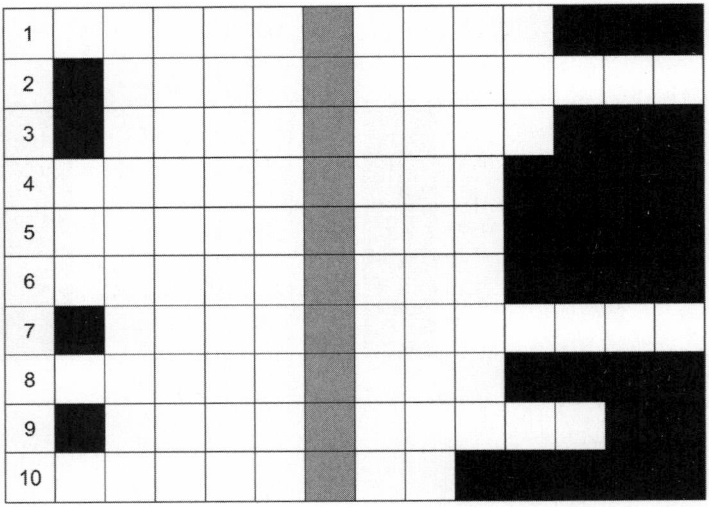

CLUES

1 UNFASTENED DRINK 5,5

2 SLENDER VEGETABLE 6,6

3 TINY SPHERE 5,4

4 MAIN PLANT BLADE 5,4

5 TRANSPARENT PERIOD OF TIME 5,4

6 DISTANT FOOT 5,4

7 LEMON MAN 6,6

8 JUVENILE ORGAN 5,4

9 AUTHORIZED BIRD OF PREY 5,5

10 EBONY PACK ANIMAL 5,3

Level 9

MEMORY CIRCLE 9

Study the grid, and remember the shapes, the words and where they are positioned. Then turn the page and answer the questions.

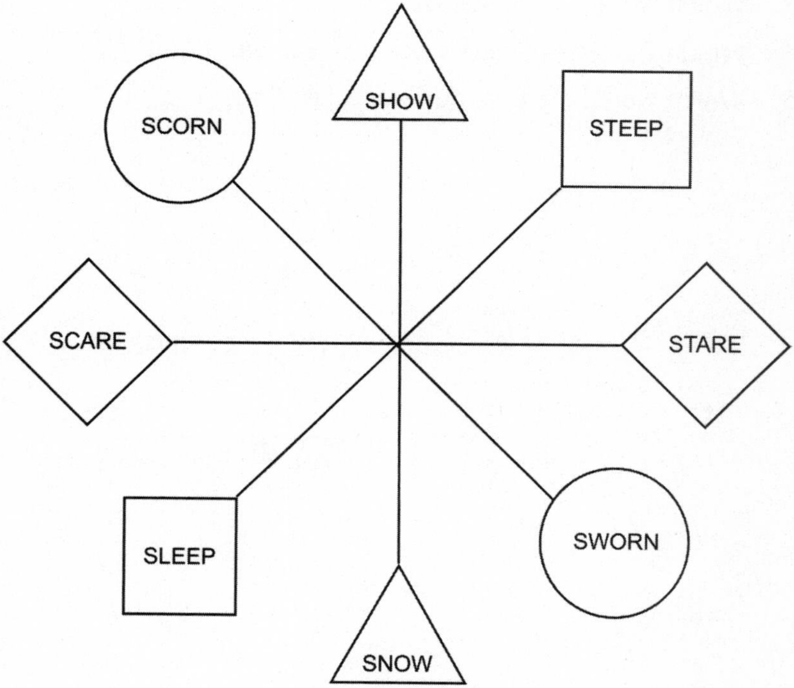

MEMORY CIRCLE 9

Questions

1. Which words have 1 vowel?
2. Which words are in squares?
3. Which word is opposite SWORN?
4. Which 2 words come between STEEP and SNOW?
5. Which word is in the south west position?

WORD CREATION 9

Taking the first letter of a 5-letter word, use it as the middle letter of a new 5-letter word. For example the word after HEATH may be USHER. Don't repeat words and avoid using proper nouns. Within 5 minutes can you create at least 40 words?

OTTER				
				40 words!

VOLVOGRAMS 9

Volvograms are words that spell another word when read backwards, for example BIN and NIB. Work out each pair of volvograms from the clues given, and then slot them into the crossword grid.

Amend text that flows (4) (4)

Dispatch a stopwatch (5) (5)

Reimbursed baby's cloth (6) (6)

TRIANGLES 9

Each triangle contains a 3-letter, 4-letter and 5-letter word, placed in the direction of the arrows. Put the words into the correct triangles.

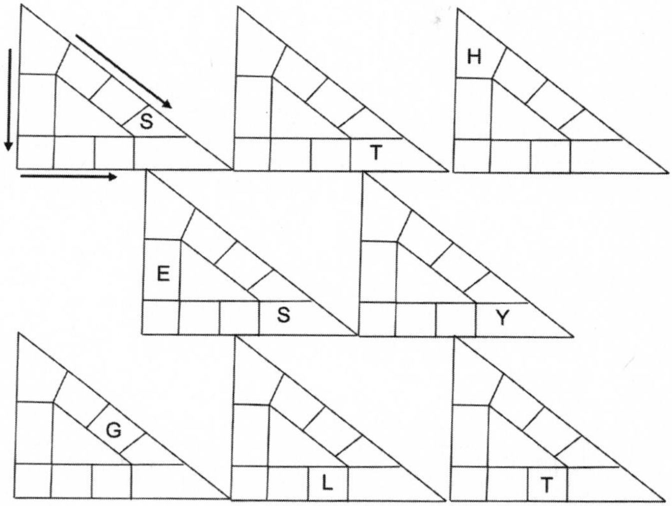

3-letter words	4-letter words	5-letter words
BAR	DUAL	BAGEL
BUD	DUTY	BALMY
BUS	RAYS	BLEAT
BUT	REST	BLESS
HAD	SAYS	HABIT
HAS	SEAT	HALLS
HER	TALL	HAPPY
HUT	TRAY	HAZEL

NINE WORDS 9

Write one or more complete sentences using words that contain the number of syllables given.

No. of letters	Sentence
1	
2	
3	
1	
2	
3	
1	
2	
3	

MARRIED WITH CHILDREN 9

Take 2 letters from each parent's name and combine them to form a 4-letter name of their child. The (m) or (f) indicates the gender. There may be more than one answer.

DIRK & FAYE (m)

ALEX & LYNN (f)

MARC & JULI (m)

OLAF & RENE (f)

AMOS & SARA (m)

LETTER CHANGE 9

Change one letter in each of the four words so that they belong to a group of similar words. The letter to change has been underlined.

ARE	ODE	OILY	SOLD

DUG	MOTH	TWIG	SUET

TENTH	STILE	LIDS	MONTH

STOW	HART	AND	SUIT

TO	NOW	LEVER	CONE

Level 9

DIAMOND WORDS 9

Find 13 words that fit the diamond grid. Avoid using the same word more than once, and words that are proper nouns.

NOTE See if you can find words that are not plurals or verb forms ending in 'S'

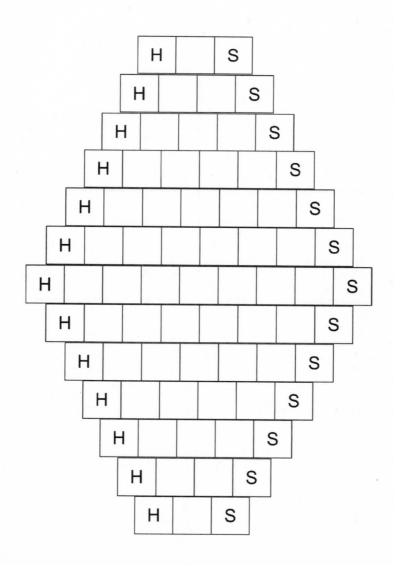

H		S						
H			S					
H				S				
H					S			
H						S		
H							S	
H								S
H							S	
H						S		
H					S			
H				S				
H			S					
H		S						

MINI WORD SUDOKU 9

Place the letters from the 6-letter word GROWTH in the grid so that each column, each row, and each of the six 2×3 sub-grids contains all of the 6 letters from the word.

W	O				
		G			O
		W			T
T			H		
G			T		
				G	H

Level 9

LETTER SHUFFLE 9

A saying has been placed in the grid in a continuous string, going from left to right, and reading from top to bottom. The 8 letters in the shaded squares have been rearranged.

The word lengths are: 2, 5, 3, 3, 2, 6, 4, 3, 2, 5

W	E	N	A	V
E	R	G	U	N
O	T	T	O	F
U	H	I	N	N
S	T	H	R	T
C	A	R	G	O
W	E	O	N	G

Saying:

____

____

____

SPEED WORDS 9

Choose 10 words that fit the criteria given. Choose words that are not proper nouns. Use a different word for each question.

Choose a word that:		
1	Contains 3 'O's	
2	Is an anagram of 'MALEBLUR'	
3	Contains the combination of letters 'SIQ'	
4	Has 5 letters in reverse alphabetical order	
5	Has 6 letters but no vowels	
6	Rhymes with 'LIZARD'	
7	Fits into _ W _ _ _ _ W	
8	Starts with 'Z' and ends with 'T' and has 2 syllables	
9	Contains 4 'E's	
10	Contains 4 'G's	

LETTER BOXES 9

Take one letter from each box to form a 5-letter word. Topic: Occupations

P M Z J B	A U I U I	Z K R L D	G S O E E	R R E E T

CLUES 9

Solve the clues then find the letters, which are placed randomly in the grid. Cross them off, circle them, or color in the square as you find them.

CLUES

1. Ocean bird (9)
2. The state of being unknown (9)
3. Signature (9)
4. Designer of buildings (9)

Y	L	N	R	Y	H
I	T	T	T	T	I
S	T	R	O	N	G
A	A	A	A	A	A
S	E	P	U	M	C
B	R	O	O	C	H

WORD PLUS WORD 9

Add a 4-letter word before the last letter so that it also makes a 5-letter word, for example STAR + E. Make each of the 4-letter words different. Avoid using proper nouns.

K				
L				
M				
N				
O				
P				
R				
S				
T				

MISSING ALPHABET 4

There are 10 words, each having a different letter of the alphabet missing. Work out which letter goes in each word. None of the words are proper nouns.

The letters are provided so you can cross off each one as you find it.

_OTEL	HOAR_	ROT_
_OARD	FLA_	WIN_
LAS_	O_EN	LAN_
	_UTE	

G J M P S V Y A D H

SQUIDS 9

Can you place the letters in the correct squares so that the grid makes 5 words that read both horizontally and vertically?

P				
	G			
		G		
			F	
				Z

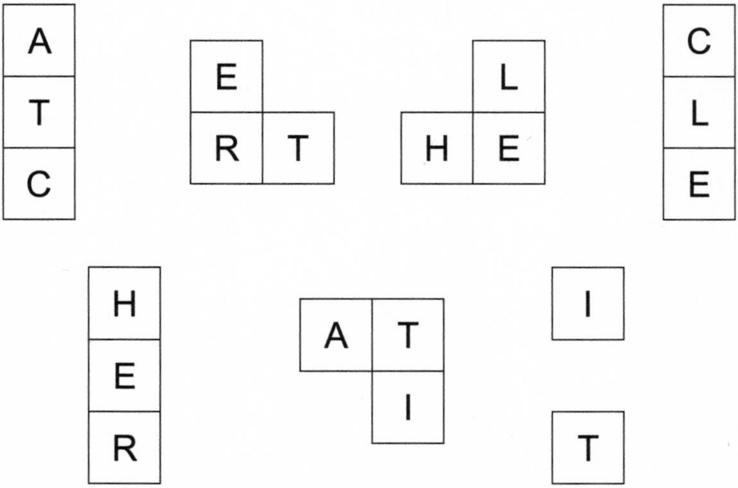

SENTENCE MAKER 9

Make up a sentence with words that fit into the structures given, where C stands for Consonant, and V stands for Vowel.

For example the sentence SHE LIKES CATS would fit into the structure CCV CVCVC CVCC. Proper nouns are allowed, and you can put punctuation anywhere in the sentence if you would like to.

C V C C ______________________

C V V ______________________

C V C C ______________________

C V ______________________

C C V ______________________

C V C C ______________________

WORKING IT OUT 9

Work out what these phrases have in common.

Science condemns psychology.

Daughters write chords.

Foreigners build castles.

Chemists doubt answers.

Ghosts watch tombs.

SYLLABLE WORDS 9

The words to find each have 3 syllables. The last syllable or section of one word forms the first syllable or section of the next, for example WONDERFUL and FULFILLING.

Starting in the centre, draw a continuous line from one word to the next. There are five words to find.

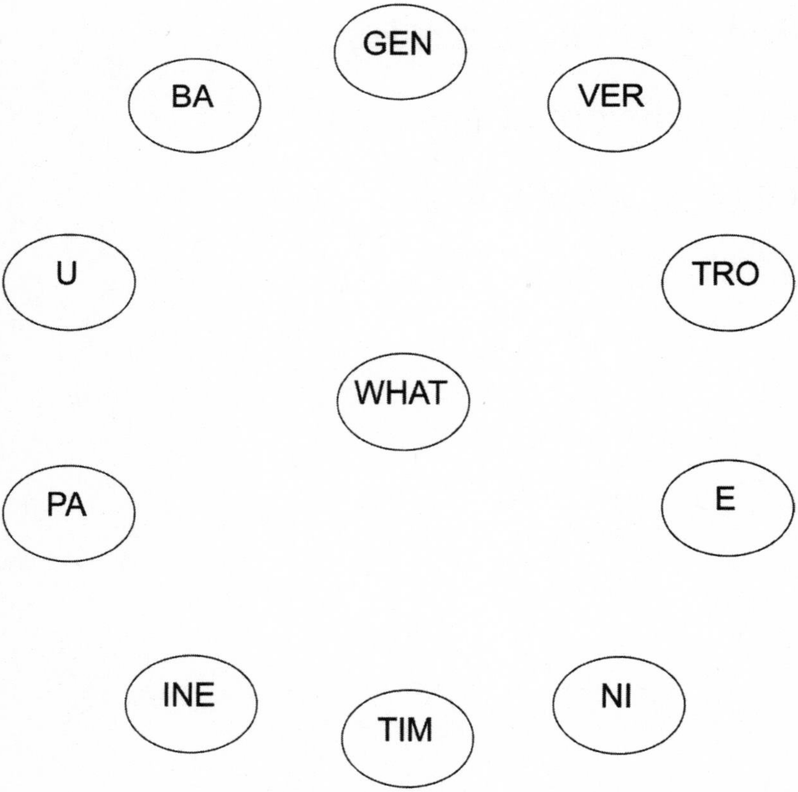

POETRY 9

Make up a limerick.

A limerick is a humorous poem consisting of a stanza of five lines, where the first, second and fifth lines rhyme with each other, and the third and fourth lines also rhyme with each other. Often the first line introduces a person or a location, which is placed at the end to establish the rhyme scheme for the second and fifth lines.

This time the last line is given:

____

____

____

____

And is now going to pull Santa's sleigh

MISSING LETTERS 9

Two letters are missing from each set of words. They are different letters for each set of words. What are the letters?

SET 1

LA_ _

CO_ _

E_ _ER

_O_ILE

SET 2

LA_ _

CO_ _

A_ _AER

_ _ILE

WORD TRAIL 9

Find the 6 words listed in the grid starting with the circled letter. The last letter of one word forms the first letter of the next word.

Note that words can also go diagonally as well as horizontally backward or forwards, or vertically upwards or downwards.

E	V	A	L	A
A	S	S	E	S
G	E	A	C	K
A	T	S	S	E
A	S	(S)	A	G

SAGES
SACKS
SALES
SAVES
SAGAS
SATES

THREE LETTERS 9

How many words can you think of that contain the three given letters in this order? They do not need to be together in the word, can occur anywhere, but need to be in this order. For example if the letters were ITE, the words could be ITEm; bITE, InnovaTE, sIsTEr, and so on.

Aim to avoid proper nouns.

You have two options here. You can spend one minute on each set of three letters, or you can choose one set of letters and spend five minutes on it.

N O N	
P H R	
P W R	
O C C	
Y E E	

Level 10

ROWS AND COLUMNS 10

Fill in the column with a word that makes the rows into complete words. There are no proper nouns used. There may be more than one answer.

A	C		E
F	L		W
M	O		E
P	I		E
B	O		T

CONCENTRATION 10

Put a circle around the words where the letters are in reverse alphabetical order

FLY	COT	ODE	ION
LID	WEB	HOW	ACE
ROD	JOY	PEA	SHE
BAG	NIB	DRY	MAD
ELM	THE	KEG	USE
WON	VOW	YAM	EAT
HEN	ASK	GYM	LEA
PLY	SEW	VET	ZIG
CAR	ILK	RUM	BET
KID	URN	MAN	TEA
ZEN	DAY	FUN	ROB
GOT	YEN	TIE	JET
SON	NEW	OLD	PIG

VOWEL WORDS 10

Choose words that fit the categories and include the given vowels.

The vowels can only be used once in the word, and must be in this order. They can be together or separate.

Vowels: **IA**	
Two boys' names	
Two girls' names	
Two place name	
Two creatures' names	
Two types of food	
Two place names	
One color	

CONTINUOUS WORDS 10

This is a list of words that have been joined together. Put the spaces in the appropriate places to work out the list of words.

DRAWNDAWDLEARROWEWERLADDERWADDLENEW
ERWANDERNOUNAWAREWARDDWINDLEOWELAWN
ROUN DWAR D E NAWEOWN ERD RAWWE DDR EWWEAR
RENOWNRENEWWENDWEEDDWELLWRENWOULDD
OWNWONDERWOODWARNANEWDEWWELDERWER
EDAWNWOUNDWORD

WORD IN WORD 10

Put the 4-letter words on the left hand side into the correct spaces to make 8-letter words.

PARE
PILE
HALE
HERO
HERE
HEAR
EARN
EARS

I	N					R	S
U	N					E	D
B					K	I	N
C					O	T	S
A	P					N	T
W					V	E	R
E					P	S	Y
R	E					S	E

WORD RHYME 10

Find as many words as you can that rhyme with the given word. Use a timer, and take a minute for each of the five words. Note that different words rhyme in different accents, so choose words that rhyme in your accent. Decide if you want to include proper nouns or not. You can include rhyming words with different spellings, for example REED and READ.

ACE	
DRESS	
DIP	
HOW	
BET	

HALF WORDS 10

Join two half words together to form seven lots of 6-letter words.

W O R	W A D
R E O	O R D
R E R	D E R
R E W	R A W
P E N	W A R
R E D	D E D
E R S	E A D

1. ____________________
2. ____________________
3. ____________________
4. ____________________
5. ____________________
6. ____________________
7. ____________________

X WORDS 10

Place the correct words in the rows in the grid so that both diagonals spell a five-letter word reading from top to bottom.

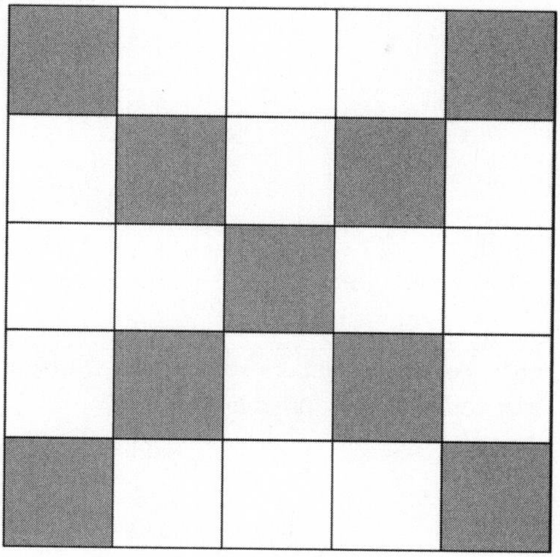

CURRY

MOTHS

FIRST

EVERY

PETTY

ALPHABET TEASERS 10

X

Find 10 words of four or five letters that end in X that are not proper nouns

Q

Find 10 words of six letters starting with Q that are not plurals, proper nouns or verb forms ending in 's'

A

Find a word for each category starting with A that fits the following criteria:

Noun with 3 syllables

Adjective with 3 syllables

Verb with 3 syllables

Adverb with 3 syllables

ANAGRAM GRID 10

Solve the anagrams and place them into the correct spaces in the grid.
Two letters have been placed for you.

SPEAR
RATES
PATER
ARRAD
TREES
CRIAD

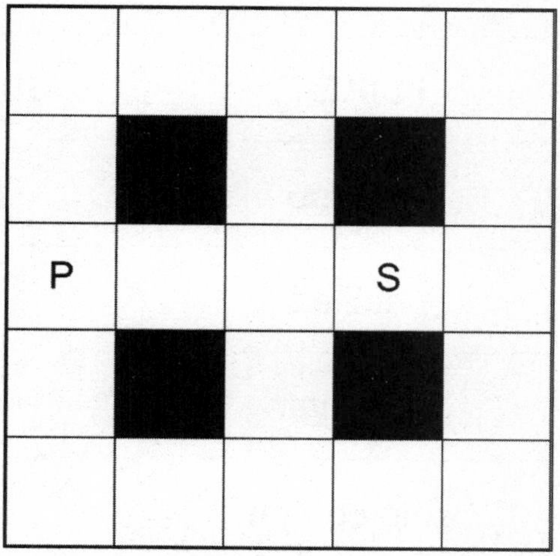

I LIKE ... 10

All the items *'I like'* have a connection that the items *'I don't like'* do not have. Can you work out the connection?

I LIKE ...	... BUT I DON'T LIKE
stylist	hairdresser
edified	taught
terminate	finish
photograph	snapshot
decide	choose
enlighten	illuminate
amalgam	combination
legible	readable

WORD FLOW 10

Think of five 6-letter words that start with the letters on the left and end with the letter in the middle. Then think of five 6-letter words that start with the letter in the middle and end with the letters on the right. Avoid using proper nouns or using the same word twice.

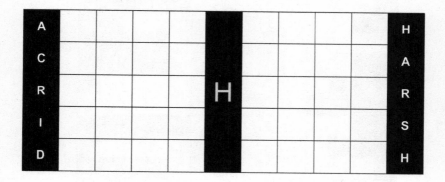

A										H
C										A
R					H					R
I										S
D										H

RHYME TIME 10

Each row in the grid contains two words that rhyme - an adjective and a noun. Solve the clues then slot the words into the grid so that the gray column also contains two rhyming words.

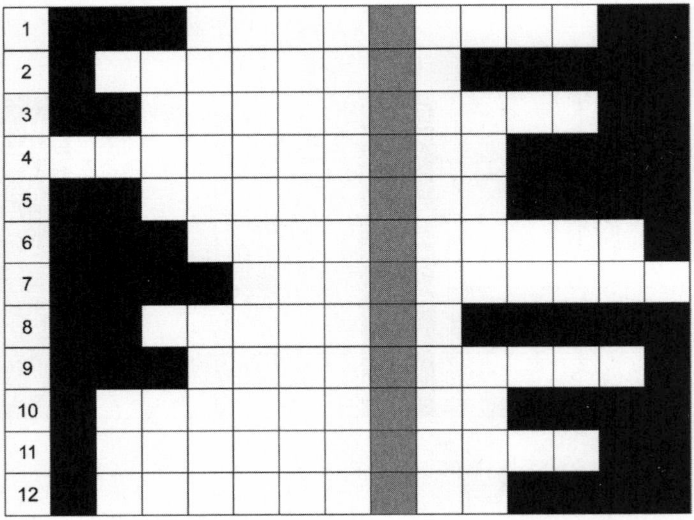

CLUES

1 COMPETENT STORY 4,5

2 DULLED INSTRUMENT 4,4

3 UNCOUTH UNWANTED GOODS 5,5

4 SPHERICAL NOISE 5,5

5 LIBERATED PLANT 4,4

6 IRRITATED DISH 5,5

7 SEVERE BOG 5,5

8 SELF SATISFIED INSECT 4,3

9 BRIEF CONTEST 5,5

10 LUXURIANT BRISTLED INSTRUMENT 4,5

11 CONVENIENT ALCOHOL 5,6

12 HELLENIC VEGETABLE 5,4

MEMORY CIRCLE 10

Study the grid, and remember the shapes, the words and where they are positioned. Then turn the page and answer the questions.

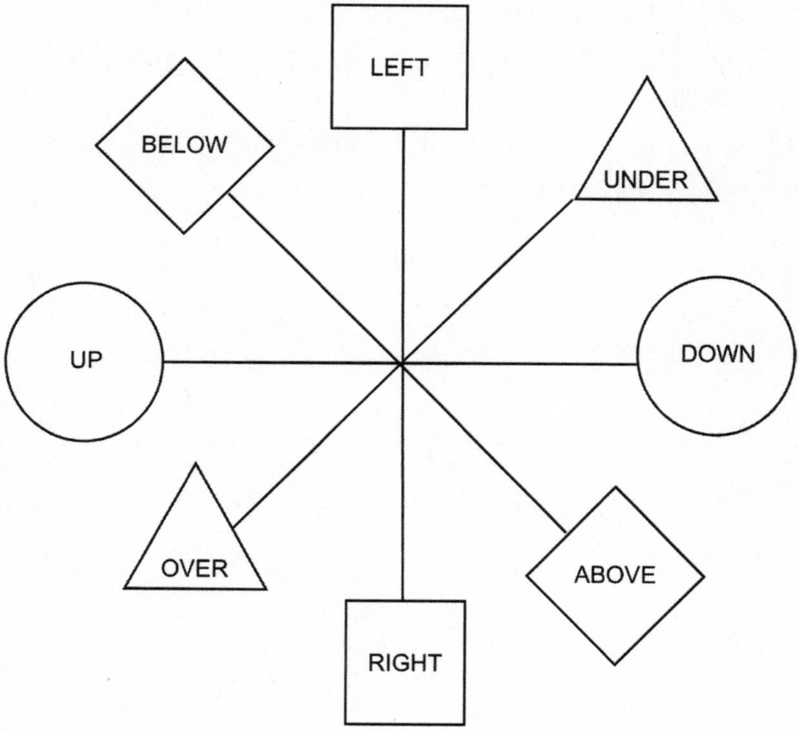

MEMORY CIRCLE 10

Questions

1. Which words are in triangles?
2. Which 2 words come between UP and UNDER?
3. Going in a clockwise direction, which word comes after UNDER?
4. Which word is in the south east position?
5. Which shape is LEFT in?

WORD CREATION 10

Taking any **three** letters from a 5-letter word, use them within a new 5-letter word. Do not use the remaining two letters. For example the word after HEALS may be SHARK but **not** SHARE. Don't repeat words and avoid using proper nouns. Within 5 minutes can you create at least 30 words?

STRAY				
				30 words!

VOLVOGRAMS 10

Volvograms are words that spell another word when read backwards, for example BIN and NIB. Work out each pair of volvograms from the clues given, and then slot them into the crossword grid.

Students' mistake (6) (6)

Hand over - berated (7) (7)

Frazzled puddings (8) (8)

TRIANGLES 10

Each triangle contains a 3-letter, 4-letter and 5-letter word, placed in the direction of the arrows. Put the words into the correct triangles.

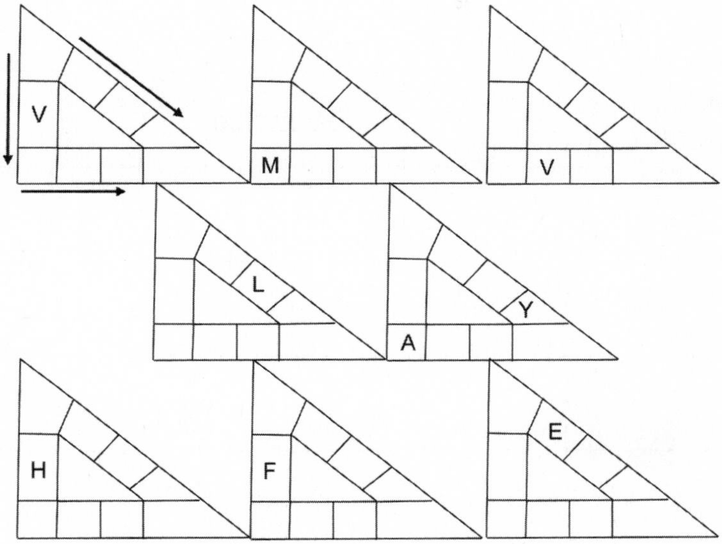

3-letter words	4-letter words	5-letter words
AFT	AXEL	ATLAS
AHA	AXIS	AVERT
AIM	EVEN	AVIAN
AVE	EXIT	AXIAL
VIA	MIEN	VALET
VIE	MINT	VEINS
VIM	TILL	VINYL
VET	TINS	VIXEN

NINE WORDS 10

Write one complete sentence using words that contain the number of syllables given.

No. of letters	Sentence
1	
2	
3	
4	
5	
4	
3	
2	
1	

MARRIED WITH CHILDREN 10

Take 2 letters from each parent's name and combine them to form a 4-letter name of their child. The (m) or (f) indicates the gender. There may be more than one answer.

LEIF & OLGA (f)	
STAN & EVIE (m)	
JOEY & FAWN (f)	
ELMO & FERN (m)	
ZANE & PINK (f)	

LETTER CHANGE 10

Change one letter in each of the four words so that they belong to a group of similar words. This time the letters to change have not been underlined!

HI	SUE	BE	WHEY

SPEAR	SHY	WELL	TALE

WIN	LEAK	ICON	BOLD

DIAMOND WORDS 10

Find 13 words that fit the diamond grid. Avoid using the same word more than once, and words that are proper nouns.

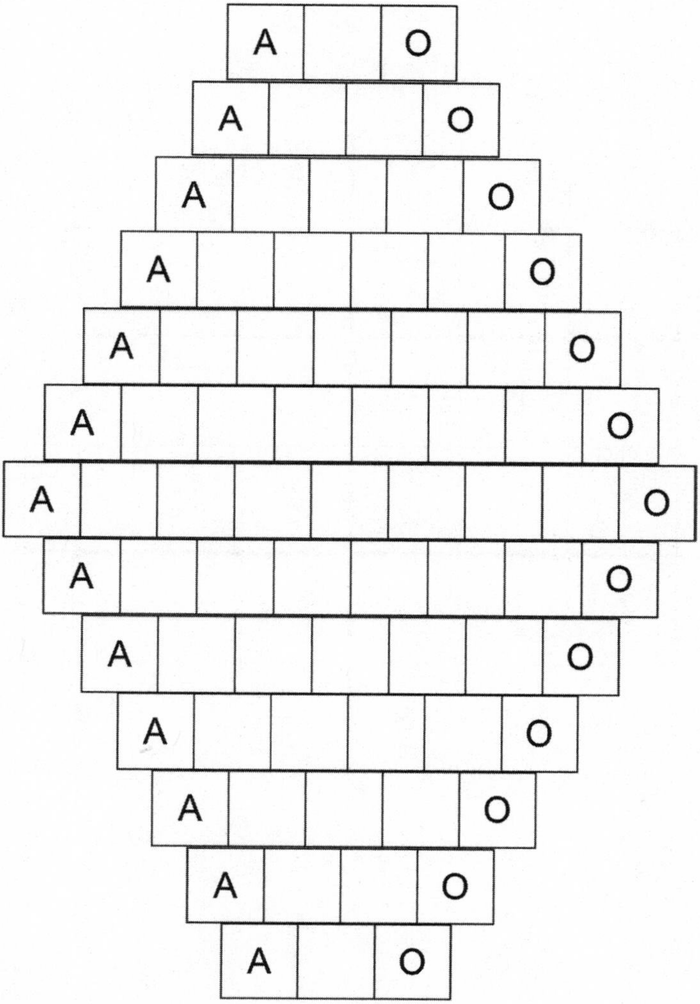

MINI WORD SUDOKU 10

Place the letters from the 6-letter word SYNTAX in the grid so that each column, each row, and each of the six 2×3 sub-grids contains all of the 6 letters from the word.

T			A	X	
					Y
	N				S
S				N	
A					
	X	S			A

LETTER SHUFFLE 10

A saying has been placed in the grid in a continuous string, going from left to right, and reading from top to bottom. The 8 letters in the shaded squares have been rearranged.

The word lengths are: 5, 2, 2, 1, 6, 5, 6, 4, 4

N	E	V	O	R
G	O	S	O	A
D	E	C	T	O
D	W	H	O	H
E	P	L	R	N
T	S	A	A	V
E	T	I	E	D

Saying:

SPEED WORDS 10

Choose 10 words that fit the criteria given. Choose words that are not proper nouns. Use a different word for each question.

Choose a word that:		
1	Is a compound word that starts with 'C' and ends with 'D'	
2	Is a 4-letter word meaning 'expensive' when the first and last letters are transposed	
3	Fits into A _ _ B _ _	
4	Ends with 'RY' and starts with 'MY'	
5	Contains 2 'A's and 2 'E's	
6	Is an anagram of 'EERYNITS'	
7	Has the combination of letters 'ESQ' but not at the beginning of the word	
8	Contains 2 'W's	
9	Fits into A _ _ _ B _ C	
10	Has 5 letters and ends with 'Z'	

LETTER BOXES 10

Take one letter from each box to form a 6-letter word. Topic: Animals

C B G C J M	E A O O A O	N D C Y U R	G O K G B K	E A T I E A	E L R Y L R

CLUES 10

Solve the clues then find the letters, which are placed randomly in the grid. Cross them off, circle them, or color in the square as you find them.

CLUES

1. Burrowing plant-eating mammal (6)
2. Gray rodent (10)
3. Large herbivorous dinosaur (10)
4. Carnivorous flying creature (4, 2, 4)

B	B	H	H	O	O
I	I	I	I	I	O
S	A	D	D	L	E
C	C	C	P	P	D
B	R	T	N	A	L
F	L	U	R	R	Y

WORD PLUS WORD 10

Add a 4-letter word before the last letter so that it also makes a 5-letter word, for example STAR + E. Make each of the 4-letter words different. Avoid using plurals and proper nouns.

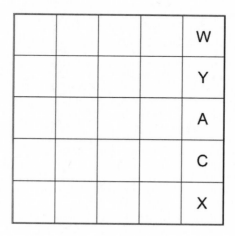

				W
				Y
				A
				C
				X

SQUIDS 10

There are 10 words, each having a different letter of the alphabet missing. Work out which letter goes in each word. None of the words are proper nouns.

The letters are provided so you can cross off each one as you find it.

_ROWN	TO_IC	_AUNT
PLAI_	SEL_	_ALLET
LIS_EN	_IRST	C_OWN
	HO_EL	

L P T X B F J N R V

SQUIDS 10

Can you place the letters in the correct squares so that the grid makes 5 words that read both horizontally and vertically?

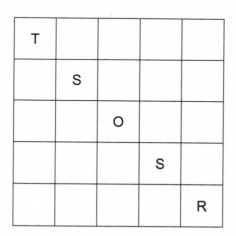

T				
	S			
		O		
			S	
				R

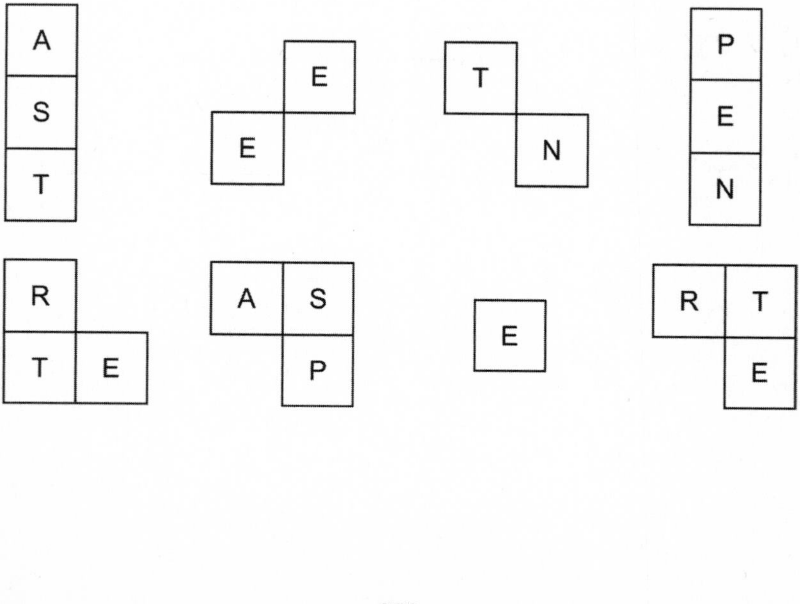

SENTENCE MAKER 10

Make up a sentence with words that fit into the structures given, where C stands for Consonant, and V stands for Vowel.

For example the sentence SHE LIKES CATS would fit into the structure CCV CVCVC CVCC. Proper nouns are allowed, and you can put punctuation anywhere in the sentence if you would like to.

C C V C V ______________________________

V C ______________________________

C C V ______________________________

C V V C V C ______________________________

C V C V C ______________________________

WORKING IT OUT 10

Work out what these phrases have in common.

Tea for two please.

I see you there.

Male knights allowed here.

We'll buy horse meat.

Find key, ring bell.

SYLLABLE WORDS 10

The words to find each have 3 syllables. The last syllable or section of one word forms the first syllable or section of the next, for example WONDERFUL and FULFILLING.

Starting in the centre, draw a continuous line from one word to the next. There are five words to find.

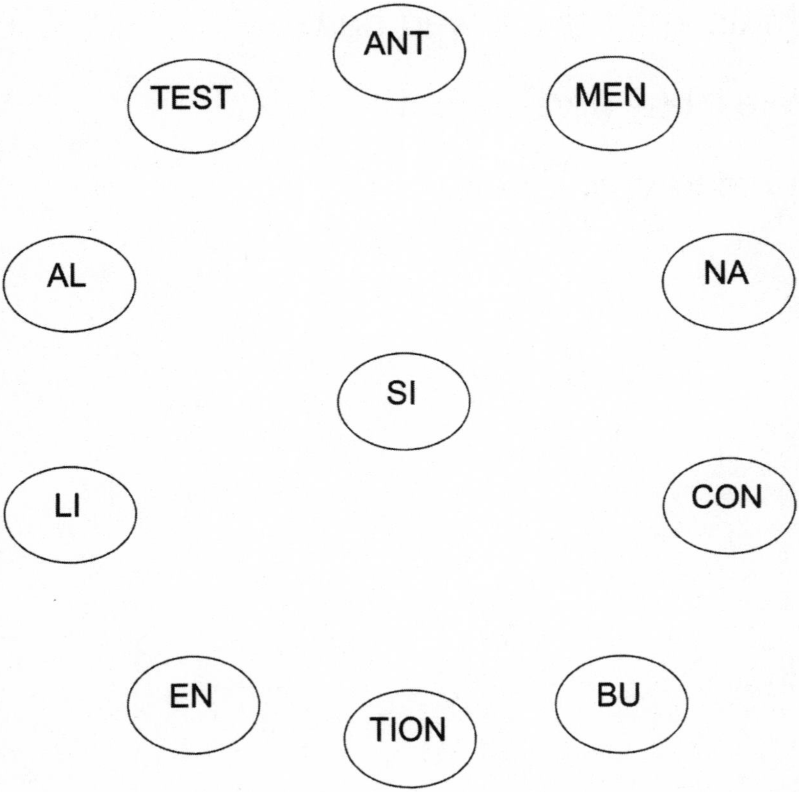

POETRY 10

Make up a limerick.

A limerick is a humorous poem consisting of a stanza of five lines, where the first, second and fifth lines rhyme with each other, and the third and fourth lines also rhyme with each other. Often the first line introduces a person or a location, which is placed at the end to establish the rhyme scheme for the second and fifth lines.

This time there are no lines given, and your task is to make up a limerick that includes all the letters of the alphabet. The letters are given below so you can cross them off as you use them.

____

____

____

____

____

A B C D E F G H I J K L M N O P Q R S T U V W X Y Z

MISSING LETTERS 10

Two letters are missing from each set of words. They are different letters for each set of words. What are the letters?

SET 1

S _ _ I N

_ N _ E L

_ E _ N L Y

S N A _ _

SET 2

S _ _ I N

C O _ _

_ E _ R N

G _ _ D E

WORD TRAIL 10

Find the 6 words listed in the grid starting with the circled letter. The last letter of one word forms the first letter of the next word.

Note that words can also go diagonally as well as horizontally backward or forwards, or vertically upwards or downwards.

E	D	A	E	S
E	S	L	M	T
S	S	A	S	A
R	A	E	E	E
E	S	P	E	(S)

SEAMS
SEATS
SEALS
SEEPS
SEARS
SEEDS

THREE LETTERS 10

How many words can you think of that contain the three given letters in this order? They do not need to be together in the word, can occur anywhere, but need to be in this order. For example if the letters were ITE, the words could be ITEm; bITE, InnovaTE, sIsTEr, and so on.

Aim to avoid proper nouns.

You have two options here. You can spend one minute on each set of three letters, or you can choose one set of letters and spend five minutes on it.

XEN	
AAA	
UDY	
ZOE	

Bonus puzzles

MISSING VOWELS 1

There are three common sayings below. The vowels and the gaps between words have been omitted. Can you work them out?

N C P N T M

B T T R L T T H N N V R

M N Y H N D S M K L G H T W R K

WORD MAKER 1

Starting with 'S', choose one letter from each column going from left to right, to form a word. Don't skip a column. Words can consist of 3 through to 6 letters.

S	A	L	A	R	T
	E	T	E	D	E
		N	I	L	Y
			T	C	

CRYPTIC H-WORDS 1

Solve the cryptic clues, and place them in the H-grid

CRYPTIC CLUES

1. One hundred and fifty always intelligent (6)
2. Intellectual donkey noise outside in (6)
3. Imagine I leave in disarray - that's difficult to understand (6)

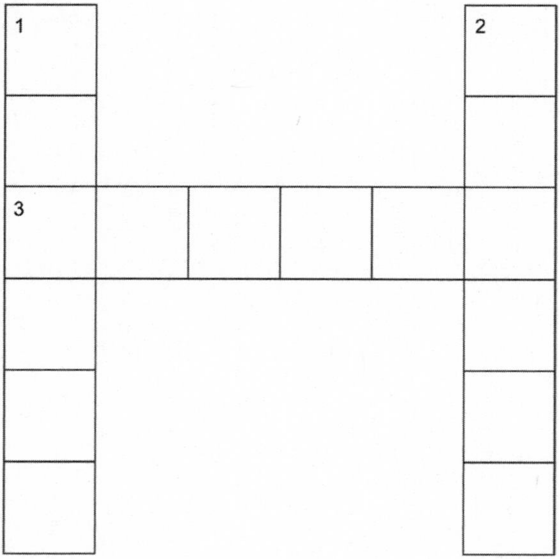

Answers

ROWS AND COLUMNS 1

R	I	**F**	T
S	H	**O**	P
P	O	**U**	R
C	A	**R**	T

CONCENTRATION 1
SEQUENCE 1: Number 4
SEQUENCE 2: Number 5

VOWEL WORDS 1
There are many acceptable answers.
Example:
ALAN, JACK; NATASHA, SAMANTHA; JAPAN, ALABAMA; CAT, PANDA; HAM, PASTA; HAT; SCARF; DARTS

CONTINUOUS WORDS 1
FLEE FLESH ISLE SELL SHELF FISH LEASH SHALE LASH FLASH SELFISH SHELL HASSLE SEAL SHALL HALF ELF AISLE FILL FLAIL FALSE SAFE FAIL FALSIFY SHY YES SALE SALSA FALL FLY HEAL LEASE LEAF SAIL YELL

WORD IN WORD 1

F	**A**	**C**	**E**	L	E	S	S
J	**O**	**U**	**R**	N	A	L	S
C	**O**	**W**	**E**	R	I	N	G
R	**E**	**V**	**E**	R	E	N	D
S	**H**	**O**	**W**	E	R	E	D

WORD RHYME 1
There are many acceptable answers.
Example:
NOSE: BLOWS CHOSE CLOSE CROWS DOZE FLOWS GOES GLOWS HOES HOSE LOWS MOWS POSE PROSE THROWS THROES
LIGHT: ALIGHT ALRIGHT BRIGHT FIGHT FLIGHT FRIGHT HEIGHT KITE MIGHT NIGHT QUITE RIGHT RITE SIGHT SITE SLIGHT TIGHT WRITE
NOTE: BLOAT BOAT COAT DOTE GLOAT GOAT GROAT MOAT QUOTE ROTE STOAT THROAT TOTE VOTE WROTE
SENT: ASCENT BENT CONTENT DENT DESCENT GENT INDENT INTENT LEANT LENT MEANT PENT RENT TENT VENT WENT
ICE: ADVICE DEVICE DICE LICE MICE NICE PRICE RICE TRICE THRICE TWICE VICE

HALF WORDS 1
AERIAL, BEHAVE, BARBER, ARISEN, ENGAGE

X WORDS 1

T	R	U	E
T	E	X	T
M	A	S	T
M	E	A	T

ALPHABET TEASERS 1
There are many acceptable answers.
Example:
D Deed deer deem deep dean deal dear doom door dais
J Jack Jon Jordan Jeffrey Jonah Jason Jacob Javed Justin Jeremy

ANAGRAM GRID 1

	A		S	
B	R	O	W	N
	R		O	
W	O	R	R	Y
	W		N	

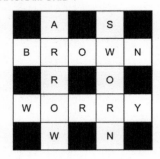

I LIKE ... 1
Words with double letters

WORD FLOW 1
There are many acceptable answers. Example:
CAROL LAYER; RIVAL LASSO; OFFAL LOBBY; WHEEL LARVA; NOVEL LEVEL

Level 1

RHYME TIME 1

1		B	I	G	F	I	G	
2	D	A	R	K	L	A	R	K
3	R	A	W	J	A	W		
4			H	O	T	P	O	T
5		T	O	P	M	O	P	
6	M	A	D	D	A	D		
7		L	O	W	T	O	E	

MEMORY CIRCLE 1

1. WHITE; 2. PURPLE, BLACK; 3. GREEN; 4. Circle; 5. PURPLE

WORD CREATION 1

There are many acceptable answers.
Example: ARNICA CARPET ETHER ERSTWHILE LEVEL ELEVEN ENTRANCE CERTAIN INCUR URGE GELATIN INSIDE DESIRE REASON ONTO TORE REPEAT ATTUNE NEST STUN UNDER ERGO GONE NEUTRAL ALTAR ARMY MYTH THROUGH GHOST STOOP OPEN ENTAIL ILLICIT ITEM EMPATHY HYDRANGEA EACH CHAIR IRKSOME MERE REST STRIPE PELLET ETHEREAL ALMOST STRAP APPROACH CHIME MENTION ONTO TOAST STALE LEAST STONE NEAT ATTIRE REGAIN INTRODUCTION ONION ONEROUS USED EDIT ITERATE TENOR ORGAN ANSWERED

VOLVOGRAMS 1

	D	A	M		
	E				
A	V	I	D		M
	I		I		A
	L	I	V	E	D
			A		

TRIANGLES 1

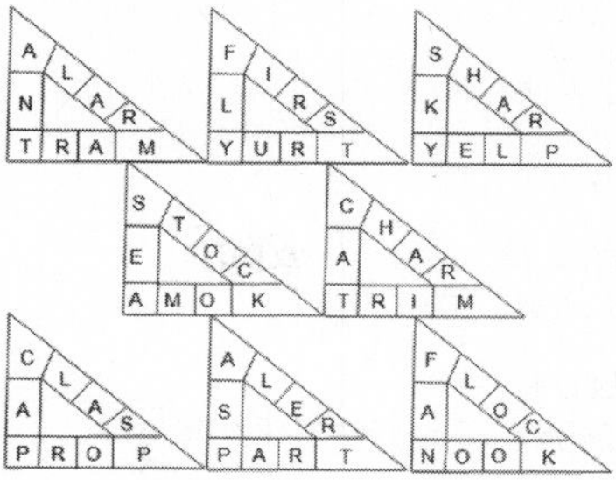

NINE WORDS 1

There are many acceptable answers.
Example:
I AM THE BEST TEXAN PLAYER, WINNING CONTESTS REGULARLY

MARRIED WITH CHILDREN 1

Answers include: STAN, DORA, ADAM, GWEN

LETTER CHANGE 1

VAST HUGE GREAT BIG BOOK NOVEL STORY TALE COOK BAKE BOIL POACH ROAD PATH LANE ROUTE

DIAMOND WORDS 1

There are many acceptable answers.
Example: SAT SEAT SHEET STREET SAWDUST SPRINT SPORT SUIT SIT

MINI WORD SUDOKU 1

E	R	W	N	S	A
N	A	S	R	E	W
S	N	E	W	A	R
A	W	R	S	N	E
R	S	A	E	W	N
W	E	N	A	R	S

LETTER SHUFFLE 1

DO NOT BELIEVE EVERYTHING YOU THINK

SPEED WORDS 1

There are many acceptable answers.
Example:
HERON, PASSIVE, PROPER, THROAT, QUIETLY, VOICE, TOXIC, SPANNER, NOVEL, KNOCK

LETTER BOXES 1

DAVE MIKE TONY GARY

CLUES 1

UNCLE ARIES LEOPARD FEBRUARY

WORD PLUS WORD 1

There are many acceptable answers.
Example: ABUT BOUT CLIP DRIP EYES FAIR GATE HAND ICON JAIL

MISSING ALPHABET 1

WINE SINK CANE CALF BOAT DEAL SHOP PACK GAIN

SQUIDS 1

M	A	S	T
A	C	H	E
S	H	O	E
T	E	E	N

SENTENCE MAKER 1

There are many acceptable answers.
Example: MY NAME IS HELEN

WORKING IT OUT 1

The words in each phrase contain the vowels A E I O U

SYLLABLE WORDS 1

CAPITAL TALISMAN MANDOLIN LINIMENT

POETRY 1

There are many acceptable answers.
Example: My mother likes to bake, She bakes from noon to night. I wish I had her skills, I can never get it right.
My cookies come out soft; The cakes are flat and tough. I think it's time to stop, And try out other stuff.

MISSING LETTERS 1

SET 1: F,R SET 2: T,L

WORD TRAIL 1

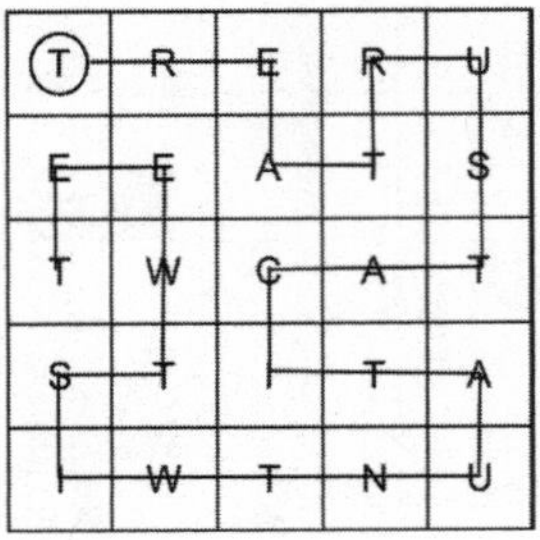

THREE LETTERS 1

There are many acceptable answers.
Example:
ART ARTIST CARROT CARAT CARET CART CHART CLAIRVOYANT DART HART HEART LARIAT MART MARTIAL MARKET MARTIN MARIONETTE TART
SIN ASSIGN SHINGLES SINE SIGN SINGING SINGER SLAPPING SLING SMILING STINK STRAPPING STAINING STRAIN SWAPPING SWING SWINGING
AIG AWNING AIMING BAKING BREAKING BERATING CRAVING CALLING CALMING CHARMING DATING DRAINING DRAWING DREAMING EASING GAMING HAVING HEALING
LAT BLEAT BLEATING BLOAT BLOATED CHOCOLATE DILATE FLAT GALLANT INFLATE INFLATION JUBILATION LEAST LAST
TOE ATONE STROKE STORE STOLE STOKE STONE STOVE TONE TONER TORE TONGUE TOLERANT TOLERATE TOWEL TROWEL

LETTER SWAP 1

SIX MEN WITH A BOY; IT'S SUNNY IN FRANCE, TAMMY

ROWS AND COLUMNS 2

S	**T**	U	N
P	**O**	U	R
A	**X**	E	D
M	**I**	N	E
S	**N**	U	B

CONCENTRATION 2

SEQUENCE 1: Number 5
SEQUENCE 2: Number 3

VOWEL WORDS 2

STEPHEN, JESSE; ELLE, HELEN; NEW JERSEY, GREECE; SHEEP, DEER; EGGS, CHEESE; VEST, BELT; CHESS

CONTINUOUS WORDS 2

LATHE AREA HEALTH THEY TALL LETTER TREE TRY REALTY THERE THREE LEATHER TELL HEAT HEART ALTER RATTLE RAY TART ALLY HEARTH RATHER TALLY YELL YEAR EARLY LYRE ALERT ETHER HALL LATER RATE TEAR TEETH TRAY

WORD IN WORD 2

A	B	S	E	N	T	E	E
S	C	R	E	A	M	E	D
T	O	P	O	L	O	G	Y
I	M	P	L	O	D	E	S
U	P	R	O	O	T	E	D
L	A	S	H	I	N	G	S

WORD RHYME 2

There are many acceptable answers.
Example:

WAIT: ATE BAIT BATE DATE EIGHT FATE FREIGHT GATE HATE IRATE LATE MATE ORATE PATE PLATE RATE SATE SLATE STATE WEIGHT
MINE: BRINE DINE DIVINE FINE KINE LINE NINE OPINE SHINE SIGN SINE
CONE: ALONE BLOWN BONE CLONE DRONE FLOWN GROAN GROWN HONE KNOWN LONE MOAN PHONE
EAT: BEAT BLEAT CHEAT DELETE FEET FLEET HEAT MEAT MEET NEAT PEAT SEAT SLEET STREET TEAT TREAT
FIVE: ALIVE ARRIVE BEEHIVE CHIVE DIVE DRIVE HIVE JIVE LIVE STRIVE

HALF WORDS 2

AIRWAY, WALLOW, LAYERS, AERATE, IMPALE, LINEAR

X WORDS 2

J	A	I	L
D	U	E	T
D	A	M	E
P	R	O	P

ALPHABET TEASERS 2

There are many acceptable answers.
Example:
B Britain's Bella Bowden's brother baked big beautiful brownies before breakfast
F Bailiff bluff cliff dandruff off sniff stuff tariff tiff whiff

ANAGRAM GRID 2

	O		T	
O	T	H	E	R
	T		E	
H	E	A	T	H
	R		H	

I LIKE ... 2

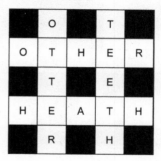

Words with three syllables

WORD FLOW 2

There are many acceptable answers.
Example: BLUNT TALKS; OVERT TOUCH; OUGHT TABOO; TWIST TWINE; SWIFT TRUSS

RHYME TIME 2

1			P	I	N	K	M	I	N	K
2		T	R	U	E	D	E	W		
3			D	O	W	N	T	O	W	N
4	W	R	O	N	G	S	O	N	G	
5		W	H	O	L	E	M	O	L	E
6				F	U	N	S	U	N	
7		L	I	M	E	D	I	M	E	

MEMORY CIRCLE 2

1. Square; 2. COLD, HOT; 3. BIG; 4. SMALL; 5. HOT

WORD CREATION 2

There are many acceptable answers.
Example: CARD AREA RENT ENOUGH NOTE OTHER THOUGH HOVER OVEN VEST ESPY SPIRE PINE INACTIVE NATION ATONE TOGETHER OGRE GREEN REVERT EVEN VERY ERA RABID ABLE BLUE LURID UREA REAP EATING ATE TEST ESPECIALLY SPIN PILFER ILIUM LIMP IMAGE MARKET ARIA RIDE IDEA DEAL EARLY ARENA RELENT ELEPHANT LEARN EAGER

VOLVOGRAMS 2

TRIANGLES 2

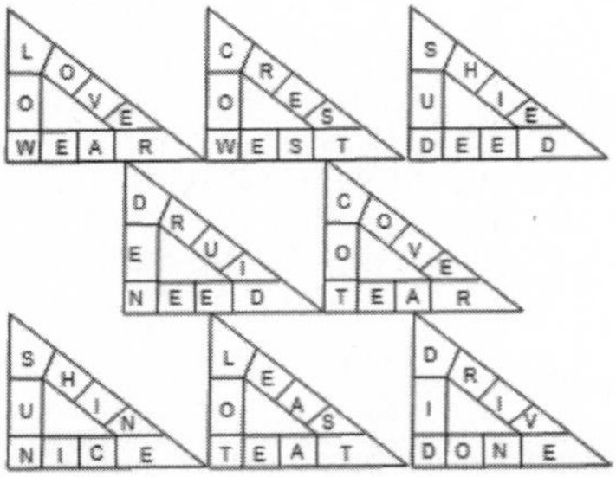

NINE WORDS 2

There are many acceptable answers.
Example:
A BORED CHILD DOESN'T EASILY FOSTER GOOD HABITS INITIALLY

MARRIED WITH CHILDREN 2

Answers include: TOBY, LUCY, NOAH, BETH

LETTER CHANGE 2

MILK WATER TEA COFFEE NORTH EAST SOUTH WEST COAT HAT GLOVE SCARF MEN WOMEN BOYS GIRLS BLUE RED PINK WHITE

DIAMOND WORDS 2

SOMETIMES WE SURVIVE BY FORGETTING
There are many acceptable answers.
Example: BAY BA BY BALMY BOUNTY BURSARY BIRTHDAY BRISKLY BUBBLY BERRY BUOY BUY

MINI SUDOKU 2

N	I	D	E	S	G
E	G	S	D	I	N
S	N	E	G	D	I
G	D	I	S	N	E
I	S	G	N	E	D
D	E	N	I	G	S

LETTER SHUFFLE 2

SOMETIMES WE SURVIVE BY FORGETTING

SPEED WORDS 2

There are many acceptable answers.
Example: TYPHOON, PRETTY, EXIST, POPPY, FURNISH, NOON, COUPLE, MYTH, AUTHOR, KAYAK

LETTER BOXES 2

TINA MARY ROSE BETH

CLUES 2

PRIDE ORANGE HEXAGON COLLEGE

WORD PLUS WORD 2

There are many acceptable answers.
Example: KILL LAND MILK NAPE OPEN PINK RAID STOP THAT UNIT

MISSING ALPHABET 2

NOSE BOOT RELY JOKE HOME QUIT LIFE STOP RACK

SQUIDS 2

T	H	I	N
H	E	R	O
I	R	O	N
N	O	N	E

SENTENCE MAKER 2

There are many acceptable answers.
Example: I LIVE IN NEW YORK

WORKING IT OUT 2

The words start and end with the same letter

SYLLABLE WORDS 2

UNIFORM FORMULA LADYLIKE LIKELIHOOD

POETRY 2

There are many acceptable answers.
Example:
I love my teacher very much, And like to do my best. This week she's always shouting, I think she's very stressed.
I've brought along an apple; Do you think that's risky? When I put it on her desk, She sighed "I just want whiskey".

MISSING LETTERS 2

SET 1: C,L SET 2: W,R

WORD TRAIL 2

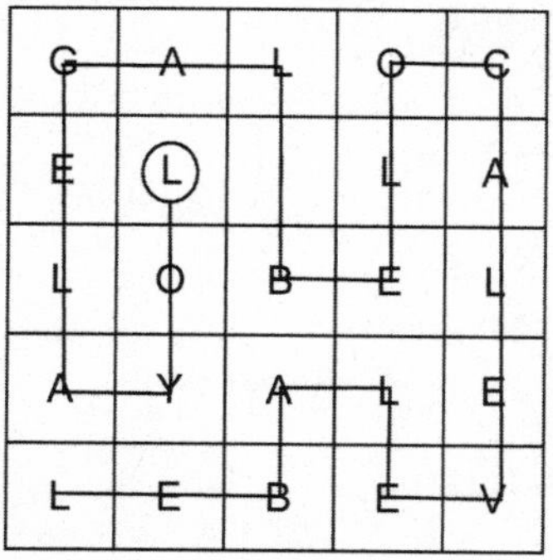

THREE LETTERS 2

There are many acceptable answers.
Example:
STR ASTER ASTRAY STRAP STRAW STRAIN STRING STRAY STRESS STRENGTH STRUCK STRIDENT STREET STREWN STRIVE STRAWBERRY STRANGE STRANGER STRANGLE
OUS CONTINUOUS CALLOUS CONTENTIOUS ENORMOUS FOCUS HEINOUS HOCUS HOUSE LOUSE MOUSE ONEROUS POROUS TOUSLE TORTUOUS REE ARRESTED CREME CREATE CREATIVE PREVIEW PRESENT PERCEIVE READER REED SCREEN TREASURE THREE
EAN BEAN CLEAN DEAN GLEAN JEANS LEAN LEANING LEARN MEAN MEANT MEANING MEANS UNCLEAN WEAN YEARN YEARNING
ACK BACK BLACK CRACKER HACK HACKLE JACK LACK PACK PACKET QUACK RACK SACK SLACK STACK SACKED SHACKLE TRACK TACK TACKLE WHACK WRACK

LETTER SWAP 2

WE LOVE YOUR HOUSE; IT'S STOKING MY BRAIN

ROWS AND COLUMNS 3

S	**T**	A	Y
D	**O**	L	L
S	**P**	I	N
W	**I**	S	E
I	**C**	E	D

CONCENTRATION 3

SEQUENCE 1: Number 6 SEQUENCE 2: Number 3

VOWEL WORDS 3

CLIFF, CLINT; KIM, LILY; FIJI, PIG; FISH, CHIPS; CHILLI; SHIRT, SKIRT; FISHING

CONTINUOUS WORDS 3

BLUSH AMUSE SHRUB BUS BUSH RUBBISH SHIRE RUSE SURE BERRY YES RUSH BURSARY MARRY RASH SHARE EAR AREA SHAM SHAME MESH SHE BRUISE RISE RUBY BRAY YEAR YAM ABUSE ARMY ASSUME BEER BRUSH MERRY SUBURB

WORD IN WORD 3

B	R	I	N	G	I	N	G
D	R	A	G	S	T	E	R
C	R	A	N	K	I	N	G
D	R	O	W	S	I	L	Y
B	R	U	N	E	T	T	E
C	R	I	N	K	L	E	D

WORD RHYME 3

There are many acceptable answers.
Example:
SHOUT: ABOUT BOUT CLOUT DOUBT FLOUT GOUT GROUT LOUT OUT POUT SNOUT TOUT
YOU: BOO CLUE DO FEW FLEW GOO GREW IGLOO JEW LOO MOO NEW OOH SUE TO TOO TWO SHOE SLEW THROUGH WHO
WHEN: DEN FEN GLEN HEN KEN MEN PEN STEN TEN THEN VENN YEN ZEN
THIS: AMISS BLISS CHRIS HISS KISS MISS SWISS
COAL: BOWL DOLE DROLL ENROL FOAL GOAL HOLE KOHL KNOLL MOLE POLE POLL ROLE ROLL SOLE SOUL STROLL TOLL TROLL VOLE WHOLE

HALF WORDS 3

ALLURE, REFILL, RESELL, PERUSE, PESTLE, PASTEL

X WORDS 3

S	H	O	W
S	N	I	P
A	N	O	N
D	R	A	W

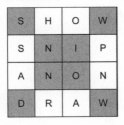

ALPHABET TEASERS 3

There are many acceptable answers.
Example:
P Peach pomegranate pear persimmon plum pineapple parsnip papaya pea pumpkin
S Seem seen seal seed seek seep seat soap soul soup

ANAGRAM GRID 3

	C		R	
C	H	E	A	T
	E		N	
T	E	A	C	H
	R		H	

I LIKE ... 3

Words starting and ending with the same letters

WORD FLOW 3

There are many acceptable answers.
Example:
HIRES SWORD; OPENS STEER; RISES SEPIA; SPINS STRAW; EMITS SHEEN

RHYME TIME 3

1	G	R	E	E	N	B	E	A	N		
2	S	I	L	L	Y	L	I	L	Y		
3	D	U	L	L	G	U	L	L			
4			N	I	C	E	R	I	C	E	
5		D	A	M	P	S	T	A	M	P	
6			R	I	C	H	W	I	T	C	H
7				S	L	O	W	C	R	O	W
8		L	O	O	S	E	M	O	O	S	E

MEMORY CIRCLE 3

1. Two: UTAH, TEXAS; 2. MAINE, TEXAS; 3. IDAHO; 4. OHIO; 5. IOWA

WORD CREATION 3

There are many acceptable answers.
Example: NOW WHY YET TOO OWN NAY YOU URN NOT TOE EAR RYE EYE EVE ELK KEY YAK KIN NIP PAT TAR RAT TWO OUR RAW WIG GNU USE EBB BAG GIN NEW WOO ORE EKE EGG GOD DOG GOO

ODD DIN NAP PAL LIP PAY YEN NIB BIN NUT TOW

VOLVOGRAMS 3

R	E	V	E	L			
O				E			B
S	U	B		V			U
E				E	R	O	S
				R			

TRIANGLES 3

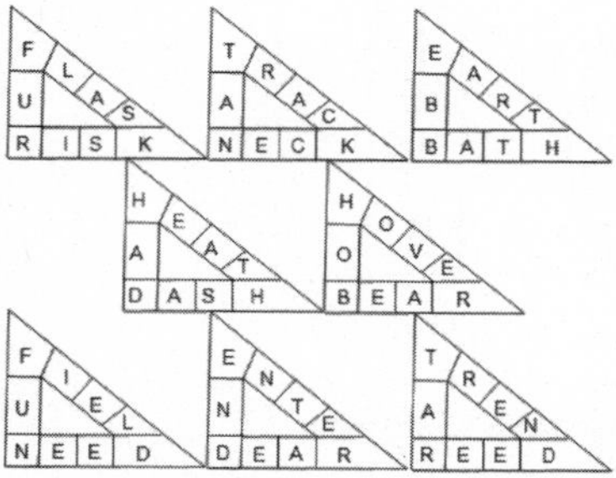

NINE WORDS 3

There are many acceptable answers.
Example:
YES, I KNOW I SHOULD BE REGULARLY MAKING MONEY

MARRIED WITH CHILDREN 3

Answers include: GINA, NEIL, JUNE, ERIC

LETTER CHANGE 3

SLIPPER SOCK BOOT SHOE CAR VAN TRUCK BUS SNOW WIND SLEET RAIN BRIDE RING GROOM VEIL WRITE LETTER PEN INK

DIAMOND WORDS 3

There are many acceptable answers.
Example: CAN CLAN CHAIN CARTON CONCERN CREATION CAPTION COTTON CLEAN CORN CON

MINI WORD SUDOKU 3

I	E	S	C	R	B
R	B	C	S	I	E
C	I	R	E	B	S
E	S	B	I	C	R
B	C	E	R	S	I
S	R	I	B	E	C

LETTER SHUFFLE 3

LIFE IS THE SCHOOL, LOVE IS THE LESSON

SPEED WORDS 3

There are many acceptable answers.
Example: PARROT, TABOO, QUIVER, ROUTE, STROLLER, GONE, RESULT, LEVEL, BICYCLE, MATTED

LETTER BOXES 3

MEAT RICE CORN FISH

CLUES 3

START SUNNY SLACK SHORTEN SYMPATHY

WORD PLUS WORD 3

There are many acceptable answers.
Example: VALE WANT XRAY YEAR ZONE ALONE BLANK CHEAT DRAFT EVENT

MISSING ALPHABET 3

QUIZ SAND TAXI HIVE POUT YEAR THEN ROWER

SQUIDS 3

L	A	M	P
A	L	O	E
M	O	V	E
P	E	E	R

SENTENCE MAKER 3
There are many acceptable answers.
Example: YOUR NEW HOUSE IS GREAT

WORKING IT OUT 3
The next word starts with the last letter of the previous word

SYLLABLE WORDS 3
PERSONAL ALIBI BICYCLE CLERICAL

POETRY 3
There are many acceptable answers.
Example:
I wish I had a cat; I'd call him Tweedledum. I'd sit him on the mat, And rub him on his tum.
I haven't got the space, To get another pet. I need another place, But that won't happen yet.

MISSING LETTERS 3
SET 1: H,T SET 2: P,D

WORD TRAIL 3

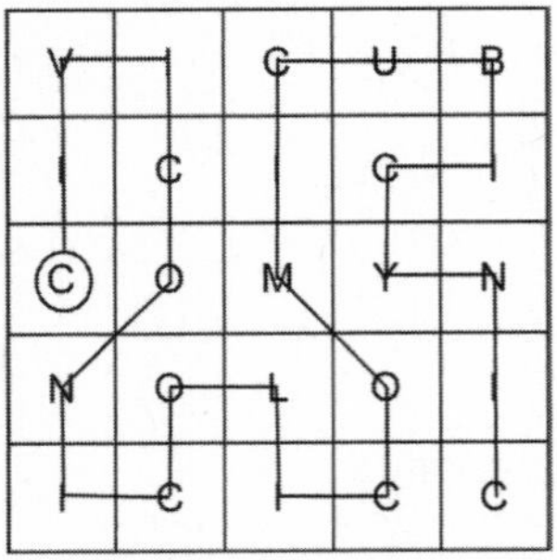

THREE LETTERS 3
There are many acceptable answers.
Example:
SHE ESCHEW SCHEME SHARE SHAPE SHED SHELTER SHELL SHEEP SHEPHERD SHIELD SHEAR SHREW SHRED
OTE BLOTTER BOTHER BOTTLE BROTHER COATED DOTE DEVOTE HOTTER JOTTED LOOTED LOTTERY MOOTED MOUTHED QUOTE ROTE ROTTEN ROTTER
IET BIGGEST FUNNIEST INDENTIFY IDENTITY INDENT QUOTIENT QUIET QUIETLY RIVET SILENT SILLIEST
ALL ALLOT ALLOW ALLOWANCE ALLEGE ALLEGATION BALL CALL FALL GALL GALLERY GALLOWS HALLOWED HALL MALL MALLET MALLOW PALL PALLID PALLIATIVE SQUALLY STALL
SSE ASSET ASSENT ASSUAGE COSSET DRESSER ESSENTIAL ESSENCE GUSSET LESSER HISSES MASSIVE MISSES PASSES RUSSET

LETTER SWAP 3
DO NOT DISCUSS WITCHES; DON'T LOSE YOUR BLACK GLOVES

ROWS AND COLUMNS 4

M	E	**S**	S
M	E	**N**	D
M	E	**E**	T
M	E	**E**	K
M	E	**R**	E

CONCENTRATION 4
SEQUENCE 1: Number 4
SEQUENCE 2: Number 5

VOWEL WORDS 4
JON, TOM; MOLLY, JODY; TOKYO, BOSTON; DOG, COW; PORK, CORN; BOOTS, SOCKS; GOLF

CONTINUOUS WORDS 4
GRAND ALARM HALL LAMP HAY GALA HARM MANY GLAND PAPAYA GANG PARAGRAPH GALL GAP PALM PAN LAND LLAMA PAGAN GLAD MAY PANG LAG HAPPY PRAY RANG HARP MALL PLAY PARRY HANGAR PALL PLAN HAND PANDA

WORD IN WORD 4

S	**E**	**V**	**E**	**R**	E	L	Y
S	**T**	**A**	**C**	**K**	I	N	G
S	**M**	**A**	**L**	**L**	E	S	T
S	**M**	**O**	**O**	**T**	H	L	Y
S	**P**	**A**	**N**	**G**	L	E	D
S	**P**	**I**	**L**	**L**	A	G	E

WORD RHYME 4

There are many acceptable answers.
Example:
KING: BRING CLING DING ICING LING MING PING RING SING SLING STING THING OWING VOTING WING WRING ZING
GREEN: BEAN BEEN DEAN E-ZINE JEAN KEEN LEAN
MAGAZINE MEAN PREEN QUEEN SCENE SEEN
SHEEN TEEN UNSEEN WEAN ZINE
HAY: BAY BRAY CLAY DAY DELAY DREY FAY FRAY
GAY JAY KAY LAY MAY NEIGH PAY PLAY PRAY RAY
SAY SLAY SLEIGH STAY STRAY
CHECK: BECK DECK HECK NECK PECK TREK WRECK
ALL: APPALL BALL BRAWL CALL CRAWL DRAWL ENTHRAL FALL GALL HALL INSTAL MALL MAUL PALL

HALF WORDS 4

ACETIC, TACKLE, AWAKEN, ACACIA, TANGLE, PENCIL

X WORDS 4

B	U	M	P
S	L	I	M
S	N	U	B
K	A	L	E

ALPHABET TEASERS 4

There are many acceptable answers.
Example:
M Mary Moore's mother, Margaret Moore, makes many marvellous macadamia muffins
V Vain vase vast veal very visa void vole volt vote

ANAGRAM GRID 4

	S		C	
C	O	U	L	D
	L		O	
L	O	C	U	S
	S		D	

I LIKE ... 4

Words where one type of vowel is used

WORD FLOW 4

There are many acceptable answers.
Example: BREAD DOING; ROUND DIVER; OOZED DANCE; WEIRD DROVE; NAMED DRAIN

RHYME TIME 4

1			B	L	A	N	D	S	A	N	D
2				G	L	U	M	C	H	U	M
3			S	L	I	M	H	Y	M	N	
4			D	R	A	B	C	R	A	B	
5		G	R	E	A	T	M	A	T	E	
6			R	E	D	H	E	A	D		
7	M	E	A	N	Q	U	E	E	N		
8	E	L	I	T	E	M	E	A	T		
9		W	E	A	K	B	E	A	K		

MEMORY CIRCLE 4

1. JUNE, AUGUST; 2. APRIL; 3. JANUARY; 4. MAY; 5. FEBRUARY, JULY, SEPTEMBER, OCTOBER, NOVEMBER, DECEMBER

WORD CREATION 4

There are many acceptable answers.
Example: SHEET THESE EVER REEL LEEK KEY YES SEEN NEVER RED DEER REEK KEEN NEW WHEN NEST TWEED DEEP PEER REED DEN NECK KEEP PERT TEE EVE EMBER RENEW WEEK KEEL LEST TELL LET TREE ERE ELK KNEW WED DEW WEST THREW WET THREE EVEN NEE ELSE ELSEWHERE EEL LENT TERN NEEDS SEWER REEF FRET THEN NEWEST TENDER REVERT TENT TWEET TEEN NEWER REMEMBER REPLETE EVERY YELL LEFT

VOLVOGRAMS 4

W	E	D		M		
		E	M	I	T	
		N		N		
	T	I	M	E		
		M		D	E	W

TRIANGLES 4

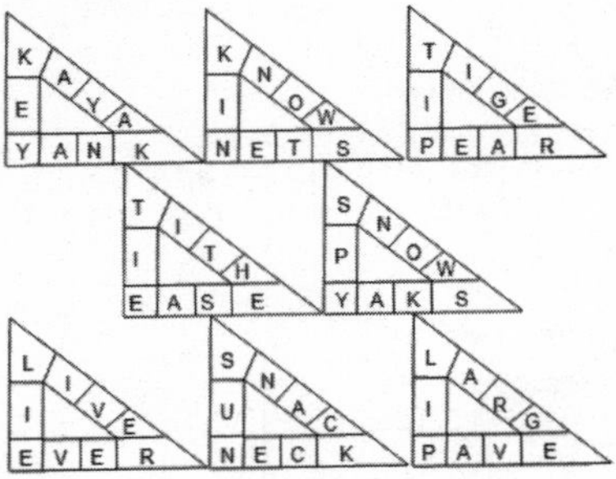

NINE WORDS 4
There are many acceptable answers.
Example: ADOLESCENT DAUGHTERS DESIRING THRILLS SHOULD OFTEN JUST SAY 'NO'

MARRIED WITH CHILDREN 4
Answers include: NOEL, DAWN, JOSH, ELLA

LETTER CHANGE 4
CHAIR SEAT SOFA COUCH WHO WHERE WHAT WHY UP DOWN LEFT RIGHT TEAR CRY SOB WEEP PLAY SCENE ACT STAGE

DIAMOND WORDS 4
There are many acceptable answers.
Example: THE TOTE TITHE TONGUE TERRACE TREASURE TWINKLE TOGGLE THERE TRUE TIE

MINI WORD SUDOKU 4

E	A	N	R	O	S
R	O	S	A	E	N
S	E	O	N	R	A
A	N	R	O	S	E
N	R	E	S	A	O
O	S	A	E	N	R

LETTER SHUFFLE 4
FALL IN LOVE WITH AS MUCH AS POSSIBLE

SPEED WORDS 4
There are many acceptable answers.
Example: ANAGRAM, ANTICIPATED, ARTIFICIALLY, CROSSWORD, BACKPACK, ERASER, LANDLADY, HARMLESS, ROWDY, LOGAN

LETTER BOXES 4
MANGO MELON PEACH LEMON GRAPE

CLUES 4
QUEEN CHICKEN PRESIDENT BUTTERFLY

WORD PLUS WORD 4
There are many acceptable answers.
Example: FRANK GLOVE HOVER IRATE JAUNT KNAVE PEACH ROVER SLASH THOSE

MISSING ALPHABET 4
RING HERO LACE CORE WORK TONE TRAM KITE

SQUIDS 4

E	A	S	T
A	V	E	R
S	E	M	I
T	R	I	P

SENTENCE MAKER 4
There are many acceptable answers.
Example: THE CAT SAT ON THE MAT

WORKING IT OUT 4
All words contain double letters

SYLLABLE WORDS 4
RITUAL ALBINO NOBLEMAN MANIFEST

POETRY 4
There are many acceptable answers.
Example:
I think I saw a rabbit; Perhaps it was a dream. It's becoming quite a habit, Where things aren't what they seem.

Is the rabbit an illusion? Did it happen in my head? It's causing me confusion. I think it's time for bed.

MISSING LETTERS 4

SET 1: T,E SET 2: H,O

WORD TRAIL 4

A	M	L	P	H
L	O	(A)	A	O
O	R	A	N	R
A	H	A	E	T
P	N	E	R	A

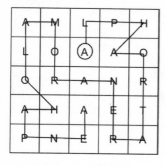

THREE LETTERS 4

There are many acceptable answers.
Example:
SCE ASCENT ESCHEW SCENE SCREAM SCREEN SCARE SCARED SCHOOLED SOCIETY SOCIETAL SACRAMENT SACRED SATCHEL SICKENED SCYTHE
CUE ACCUSE CRUEL CRUET CURE CURED CURSE COURSE CRUMBLE CURDLE CAUSE CLUE CHUTE CLUELESS SECURE SECURED SCOURGE
ONG ALONG AMONG BELONG DONG DONGLE DONATING GONG HOPING LONG LONGER MOVING MOWING OWING PRONG ROVING SONG SARONG THRONG
ETY ENTITY ENMITY JETTY MERITOCRACY MONETARY NOTORIETY PIETY PROPERTY PRETTY PETTY SWEATY TENACITY TERRITORY
TTE BETTER BATTLE BATTER BRITTLE CATTLE CUTTLEFISH DOTTED FETTLE FITTER GUTTED GUTTER HOTTER JUTTED JOTTER LATTER MATTER NATTER OTTER PATTER PRATTLE

LETTER SWAP 4

ELSA LIGHTS FIRES; I GAVE TEN RAPS, HAL

ROWS AND COLUMNS 5

T	E	**L**	L
T	E	**E**	M
T	E	**A**	M
T	E	**R**	M
T	E	**N**	T

CONCENTRATION 5

SEQUENCE 1: Number 4 SEQUENCE 2: Number 5

VOWEL WORDS 5

KURT, GUY; RUTH, JUDY; CYPRUS; DUCK, BULL; NUT, PLUM; ZULU; DRUMS

CONTINUOUS WORDS 5

SEVEN DEPEND ELDER EVEN ELEVEN SEND LEPER NERVE PEN REED DEER REPEL SEER LEVEE LESSEN PEEL SEED LEVEL DRESS RED SERVE SENSE PRESS NEVER SEEN SEVER RENDER SERENE PEEP SNEER VEER SPREE VENEER PEER VERSE

WORD IN WORD 5

A	**B**	**A**	**N**	**D**	O	N	S
A	**M**	**A**	**T**	**E**	U	R	S
A	**P**	**E**	**R**	**T**	U	R	E
A	**L**	**I**	**E**	**N**	A	T	E
A	**M**	**E**	**N**	**D**	I	N	G
A	**C**	**H**	**I**	**N**	G	L	Y

WORD RHYME 5

There are many acceptable answers.
Example:
ON: CON DON EON GONE JOHN NONE ONE RON SHONE SWAN YON
KEY: BE BEE FEE FLEA FLEE FREE GLEE HE GEE KNEE LEA LEIGH ME PEA SEA SEE SHE TEA TEE THREE TREE WE

SNOW: AGO BLOW DOUGH FLOW FRO GLOW GO GROW HOE JOE LOW MOW NO OH RHO SEW SO SOW TOE TOW WHOA YO
EYE: BUY BY BYE CRY DIE DRY FLY FRY HIGH LIE LYE MY NIGH PI PIE RYE SHY SIGH SPY STY TIE TYE VIE WHY
LONG: ALONG BELONG DONG FURLONG GONG PONG PRONG SONG STRONG WRONG

HALF WORDS 5
LACTIC, LICHEN, PICKET, CAPTOR, TIRADE, DECIDE

X WORDS 5

S	L	A	B
S	H	O	P
T	A	I	L
T	R	A	P

ALPHABET TEASERS 5
There are many acceptable answers.
Example:
G Haggle hugged blogging bragging rugged giggle gaggle woggle wiggle flogged
I Iris Irina Ida Isla Iona Irene Isobel Isabella Imogen India N Nice neat new naughty noble narcissistic nebulous nefarious negligible noticeable

ANAGRAM GRID 5

	S		T	
C	H	A	R	T
	A		A	
E	R	A	S	E
	E		H	

I LIKE ... 5
Words with one vowel

WORD FLOW 5
There are many acceptable answers.
Example: SOUTH HAREM; PERCH HELLO; EARTH HAVEN; NORTH HORSE; DITCH HOLLY
Words with one vowel

RHYME TIME 5

1	S	N	I	D	E	B	R	I	D	E	
2			F	A	I	R	H	A	I	R	
3		F	O	W	L	O	W	L			
4	F	R	A	I	L	W	H	A	L	E	
5		P	L	A	I	N	C	H	A	I	N
6		W	I	L	D	C	H	I	L	D	
7			R	E	A	L	M	E	A	L	
8	C	U	T	E	B	O	O	T			
9			S	L	O	W	S	N	O	W	
10		C	L	E	A	N	T	E	E	N	

MEMORY CIRCLE 5
1. MELON, LEMON; 2. GRAPE; 3. FIG; 4. LEMON, PEACH; 5. GRAPE, PEAR

WORD CREATION 5
There are many acceptable answers.
Example: LEVER VOTER TONER NEVER VISOR SORRY RISER SLING IRONS OTHER HERON RIDER DOTES TWEED EVENT ENTER TOAST AVERT ELECT EVADE ABOUT OVERT EMPTY POSER STRIP ROSES SNACK ALOOF OUTER THREE RELAY LAYER YIKES KAYAK YOLKS LINER NOOSE OGRES RABID BALMY LISPS SUNNY NAILS IRATE ABACK ACIDS IDOLS OVALS ALERT EVERY EMITS ICONS ORATE ABOUT OTTER

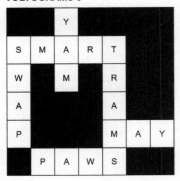

VOLVOGRAMS 5

		Y				
S	M	A	R	T		
W		M		R		
A				A		
P				M	A	Y
	P	A	W	S		

TRIANGLES 5

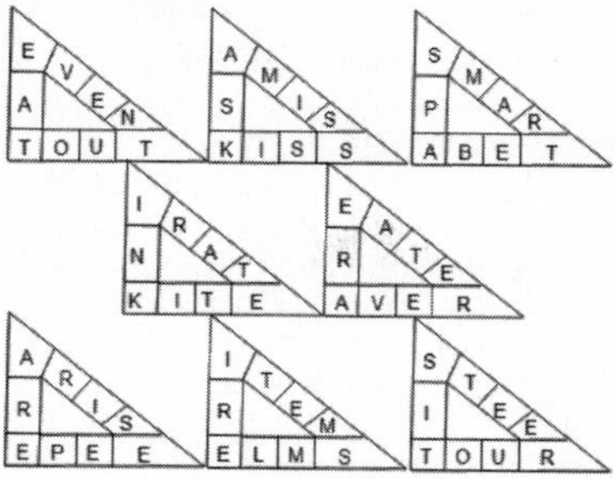

NINE WORDS 5

There are many acceptable answers.
Example:
HE'LL BE THERE NEXT WEEK WHEN THEY'RE SET FREE

MARRIED WITH CHILDREN 5

Answers include: EMMA, ALAN, JEAN, MARK

LETTER CHANGE 5

TREE BUSH SHRUB GRASS LAKE POND SEA CANAL CAT DOG BIRD FISH MOM SISTER AUNT GRAN DAY WEEK MONTH YEAR

DIAMOND WORDS 5

There are many acceptable answers.
Example: PAR PEAR POKER PLAYER PAINTER PRISONER PLASTER PAMPER POWER PEER PER

MINI WORD SUDOKU 5

N	I	K	E	Z	A
Z	A	E	N	K	I
A	Z	I	K	N	E
K	E	N	I	A	Z
E	N	A	Z	I	K
I	K	Z	A	E	N

LETTER SHUFFLE 5

AIM TO BE HUMBLE AS YOU COULD BE WRONG

SPEED WORDS 5

There are many acceptable answers.
Example: STAUNCH, BRAINY, CONQUER, QUANGO, UNUSUALLY, BILLBOARD, SHINE, OBOE, COFFEE, CHROME

LETTER BOXES 5

TIGER BISON TAPIR CAMEL LEMUR

CLUES 5

LIGHT TWIST PRETTY VIOLENT VIBRANT

WORD PLUS WORD 5

There are many acceptable answers.
Example: LEARN MUSED NEVER ORATE USAGE VOWED WINCH YEARN

MISSING ALPHABET 5

FURY RASH HARD JOIN BRINE REFER THINK HELL TRAP

SQUIDS 5

S	T	O	W
T	U	N	A
O	N	L	Y
W	A	Y	S

SENTENCE MAKER 5

There are many acceptable answers.
Example: GRAN GAVE JIM A BIG KISS

WORKING IT OUT 5

Words contain letters that are symmetrical vertically

SYLLABLE WORDS 5

DYNAMO MOCCASIN SINISTER TERMINATE

POETRY 5

There are many acceptable answers.
Example:
Spring flowers blossom And bring color to our life; A picture of joy.

MISSING LETTERS 5

SET 1: S,N SET 2: G,T

WORD TRAIL 5

R	E	C	Y	E
A	A	R	O	R
D	A	E	(R)	I
O	R	S	D	E
W	E	R	I	R

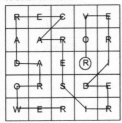

THREE LETTERS 5

There are many acceptable answers.
Example:
QUA EQUAL EARTHQUAKE EQUALITY QUASH QUARK QUAKE QUALITY QUANTITY QUANTIFY QUAFF QUANGO QUARREL SQUASH SQUAW SQUABBLE SQUARE
NNE ANNEX ENGINE ENHANCE ENTRANCE INNOVATE INNOCENT LINNET NONE NINE SONNET UNNERVING
OOR BOOR BLOOPER COMMONER DOOR FOLLOWER FLOOR MOOR POORLY ROOFER
DAY DAISY DAILY DALLY DAINTY DAMNATORY DAYTIME DAYLIGHT DAIRY DIARY TODAY YESTERDAY
IDE ASIDE BIDE BRIDE BIDDER BIDDEN CHIDE COLLIDE DECIDE DIVIDE DERIDE GRIDDLE GUIDE HIDE MIDDEN MIDDLE PRIDE SIDE STRIDE SLIDE TIDE

LETTER SWAP 5

LARA WAITS AT THE CASTLE; I REAR BOYS AND CATS

ROWS AND COLUMNS 6

C	O	**S**	T
C	O	**P**	Y
C	O	**I**	N
C	O	**L**	D
C	O	**L**	T

CONCENTRATION 6

"July is the better month" June said, "that is, without doubt, when we should meet."

VOWEL WORDS 6

ANDREW; ANNE; FRANCE; SNAKE ; APPLE, CAKE; JACKET; ARCHERY

CONTINUOUS WORDS 6

BOLD DOLL OLD DONOR BROOM LOOP BORON MOOD POLL DOOR NOOK BORN PLOD LOOM MONK BROOK DODO MOOR LOOK MOON ODD PORK BOOM NORM DROOP PROD ROOK POLO DOOM BOOK POOL PROP DROOL ROOM BOON

WORD IN WORD 6

S	**H**	**A**	**C**	**K**	L	E	D
S	**P**	**A**	**C**	**E**	M	A	N
B	**R**	**A**	**C**	**E**	L	E	T
P	**L**	**A**	**N**	**K**	T	O	N
C	**R**	**A**	**C**	**K**	E	R	S
P	**L**	**A**	**C**	**E**	B	O	S

WORD RHYME 6

There are many acceptable answers.
Example:
SELL: BELL BELLE CELL DELL FELL GEL HELL KNELL NELL QUELL SHELL SWELL TELL UPSELL WELL
BACK: BLACK CRACK FLACK FLAK HACK JACK KNACK LACK MAC PACK QUACK RACK SACK SLACK SNACK STACK TACK TRACK WHACK WRACK YAK
FEED: BEAD BEDE BLEED CEDE DEED FREED GREED HEED INDEED LEAD MEAD NEED READ REED SEED STEED TWEED WEED AIM: BLAME CAME CLAIM DAME FAME FLAME FRAME GAME LAME MAIM NAME SAME SHAME TAME
SIZE: ARISE CRIES FLIES LIES PRISE PRIZE RISE SHIES SIGHS SPIES SURPRISE THIGHS UNWISE VIES WISE

HALF WORDS 6

IDEALS, DECADE, ACIDIC, ASSESS, LABELS, STABLE

X WORDS 6

P	R	O	N	G
B	E	R	R	Y
C	L	A	S	S
S	P	A	C	E
E	A	R	T	H

RHYME TIME 6

1	V	I	L	E	P	I	L	E		
2			T	H	I	N	C	H	I	N
3	T	A	M	E	N	A	M	E		
4	B	L	A	C	K	S	A	C	K	
5		H	A	R	D	G	U	A	R	D
6		D	E	A	R	B	E	E	R	
7	I	L	L	P	I	L	L			
8			K	I	N	D	M	I	N	D
9	S	L	I	C	K	B	R	I	C	K

ALPHABET TEASERS 6

There are many acceptable answers.
Example:
E Essence eventuate elegance effective cheese sneeze breeze delete degree needle
K Knight knock knell knife know knowledge knack knave knee knit
W Wallaby walrus warthog wasp warbler weasel whale wolf wombat wren

MEMORY CIRCLE 6

1. Triangle; 2. SIX; 3. NINE, TWO; 4. Diamond; 5. FIFTY, EIGHTY

WORD CREATION 6

There are many acceptable answers.
Example: LEAP TELL LILY TINY LINE NEST STOP POLL PLAY LEAD DECK CARD RIDE DARN NODE NECK RICE RING GRAY GORE REAL LAMP PRAY RIPE PINK KEEP DEER AREA PARK RINK NEAR AXLE LAST SLIP LION NINE SENT SIGN GOES RAGE GAIN INTO TORE REAL LACK CLIP PITY TILL LOST SOUP PUNT TRIP TRAY

ANAGRAM GRID 6

	H		S	
E	A	R	T	H
	T		A	
H	E	A	R	T
	S		E	

VOLVOGRAMS 6

			G			
S	T	R	A	P		
	O		R		P	
	P		B	R	A	G
					R	
			P	O	T	
					S	

I LIKE ... 6

Words containing letters from the first half of the alphabet

WORD FLOW 6

There are many acceptable answers.
Example: SWERVE ENDEAR; TIRADE EMERGE; ORNATE EMBOSS; PIRATE EXPORT

MARRIED WITH CHILDREN 6

Answers include: IVAN, ROSE, DAVE, ZENA

LETTER CHANGE 6
FISH GILL SWIM SCALES PEACH PEAR PLUM GRAPE HEAR SEE SMELL TOUCH COW SHEEP PIG GOAT DUSK DAWN DAY NIGHT

TRIANGLES 6

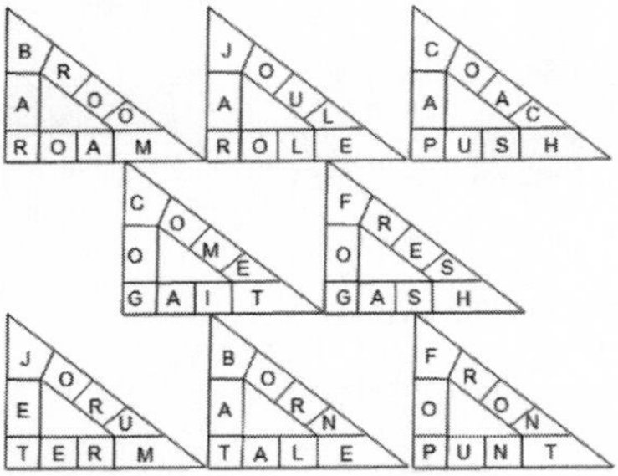

NINE WORDS 6
There are many acceptable answers.
Example: BIG JOE AND WEE AMY HAD TEA FOR TWO

MARRIED WITH CHILDREN 6
Answers include: IVAN, ROSE, DAVE, ZENA

LETTER CHANGE 6
FISH GILL SWIM SCALES
PEACH PEAR PLUM GRAPE
HEAR SEE SMELL TOUCH
COW SHEEP PIG GOAT
DUSK DAWN DAY NIGHT

DIAMOND WORDS 6
There are many acceptable answers.
Example: HID HEED HOARD HORRID HAUNTED HYDRATED HOMESTEAD HAPPENED HUMBLED HALTED HONED HERD HAD

MINI WORD SUDOKU 6

N	I	T	C	A	O
O	C	A	I	N	T
C	O	N	A	T	I
A	T	I	N	O	C
T	N	C	O	I	A
I	A	O	T	C	N

LETTER SHUFFLE 6
SMILE TODAY, TOMORROW COULD BE WORSE

SPEED WORDS 6
There are many acceptable answers.
Example: CHOICE, ELEVEN, EMERGE, FUNGI, AMONG, EIGHT, ZIGZAG, QUALIFIED, PAMPER, INGESTING

LETTER BOXES 6
CONGO KOREA CHILE NEPAL TIBET

CLUES 6
CLOSE RECEPTIONIST PERFECTIONIST

WORD PLUS WORD 6
There are many acceptable answers.
Example: SAGA CARD CANE SING WITH TAXI PARK PEAL WARM

MISSING ALPHABET 6
LUSH AWAY FLEX SHIP LADY RATE QUIP SWAY VIEW

SQUIDS 6

P	L	A	N
L	I	C	E
A	C	E	S
N	E	S	T

SENTENCE MAKER 6
There are many acceptable answers.
Example: THIS IS MY BEST FRIEND

WORKING IT OUT 6
Words contain letters that are from the top line of a QWERTY keyboard

SYLLABLE WORDS 6
ATROPHY PHYSICAL CALICO CORONA

POETRY 6
There are many acceptable answers.
Example:
It helps to know that Clouds have a silver lining; This gives people hope.

MISSING LETTERS 6

SET 1: C,L SET 2: H,R

WORD TRAIL 6

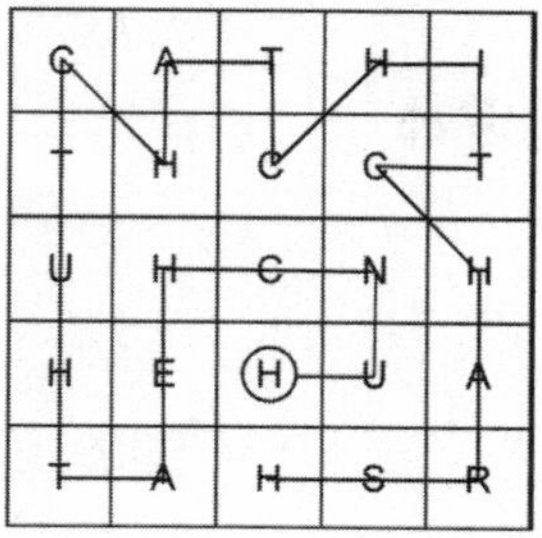

THREE LETTERS 6

There are many acceptable answers.
Example:

AAR AVATAR AWARE AVARICE AJAR AFAR CANARY CALENDAR IMAGINARY MANAGER SALAMANDER VAGARY

MOO IMPOSITION MOON MOOD MOONLIGHT MOODY MOTION MOOR MOORING MOOSE SMOOTH

MAN BEMOAN HUMAN HUMANE HUMANITY MANAGER MANACLE MANDATE MANGER MEAN MEANT MOAN

RLY AURALLY BURLY CURLY DEARLY DRILY EARLY HOURLY NEARLY OVERLY OVERTLY ORALLY POORLY RALLY REALLY RAILWAY RELY REPLY SURELY

HOE HOSE HOPE HONE HOLE HOBBLE HORSE HOUSE HOOKED HOODED HONED SHOE SHORE SHONE THOSE THRONE THROES WHOLE

ROWS AND COLUMNS 7

P	A	**C**	E
P	A	**I**	L
P	A	**V**	E
P	A	**I**	D
P	A	**C**	K

CONCENTRATION 7

How many capital letters in the passage? 9
How many two-letter words in the passage? 18 How many letter E's in the passage? 61

VOWEL WORDS 7

ROBERT; ROSE; ROME; HORSE; HONEY; GLOVES; POKER

CONTINUOUS WORDS 7

ATTIC CACTI NATION COIN CARROT AORTA TACT NOON ANTIC COAT INTO CANNON ROOT CONTACT TACO TACIT ROTA CORN TOOT CARTOON ACTOR TACTIC ROTATION CROON ACTION TONIC TRACTOR RATION TROT CORD CART TORT TRACTION ROTOR TORN

WORD IN WORD 7

U	N	**O**	**P**	**E**	**N**	E	D
L	I	**S**	**T**	**E**	**N**	E	D
E	L	**E**	**V**	**E**	**N**	T	H
S	L	**O**	**V**	**E**	**N**	L	Y
R	E	**D**	**E**	**E**	**M**	E	D
F	L	**A**	**M**	**E**	**N**	C	O
E	S	**T**	**E**	**E**	**M**	E	D

WORD RHYME 7

There are many acceptable answers.
Example:

LEEK: BEAK CREAK EEK FREAK GREEK LEAK MEEK PEAK PEEK PIQUE REEK SEEK SLEEK SPEAK TEAK TWEEK WEAK WEEK WREAK

HIDE: ABIDE BIDE BRIDE CHIDE COLLIDE DRIED FRIED GUIDE HIDE LIED NIDE PRIDE RIDE SIDE SHIED SLIDE STRIDE TIDE TRIED WIDE

LANK: BANK BLANK CRANK DANK DRANK FLANK FRANK HANK PLANK PRANK RANK SANK SHANK SHRANK STANK TANK THANK YANK

END: BEND BLEND DEPEND FEND FRIEND LEND MEND SEND STIPEND SUSPEND TEND WEND

ROUND: ABOUND AROUND BOUND BROWNED CROWNED DROWNED FROWNED GROUND HOUND MOUND POUND SOUND WOUND

HALF WORDS 7

COARSE, COCOON, COHERE, FALCON, MASCOT, COMMON

X WORDS 7

B	L	E	S	S
M	O	C	H	A
B	R	O	W	N
T	E	N	T	H
S	P	I	N	S

ALPHABET TEASERS 7

There are many acceptable answers.
Example:
O Polo foregone pogo porous cotton hollow hologram follow coroner motor
R Refer rover rider remember river ranger rapper runner rudder rigger
Z Buzzer dazzle embezzle fizz jazz muzzle nuzzle puzzle quizzical whizzed

ANAGRAM GRID 7

	S		S	
A	N	K	L	E
	A		A	
S	K	A	T	E
	E		E	

I LIKE ... 7

Palindrome words (words that read the same backward or forward)

WORD FLOW 7

There are many acceptable answers.
Example: TENDER RHYTHM; APPEAR RUNWAY; LETTER REGENT; EDITOR RADISH

RHYME TIME 7

1		R	U	D	E	F	O	O	D			
2	B	E	T	T	E	R	L	E	T	T	E	R
3		T	E	N	S	E	F	E	N	C	E	
4			F	U	N	N	Y	B	U	N	N	Y
5			S	L	A	C	K	S	H	A	C	K
6		B	R	I	G	H	T	L	I	G	H	T
7		V	A	S	T	B	L	A	S	T		
8		B	R	A	V	E	G	R	A	V	E	
9	W	H	I	T	E	N	I	G	H	T		
10				L	A	C	E	R	A	C	E	
11			H	I	G	H	S	K	Y			

MEMORY CIRCLE 7

1. BEAR; 2. RABBIT, HARE; 3. MOUSE; 4. Diamond, DEER; 5. DOG, CAT

WORD CREATION 7

There are many acceptable answers.
Example: PAIL TRAP HART PATH TRIP LAST HAIL DISH LEND WILL FLOW SELF TOES SEAT WINS SHOW GUNS SING HOPS BATH LAMB MALL FARM HOOF LASH DIAL LAID WAIL DHOW HARD DASH SEND PINS SHIP TIPS MEET ROOM MOOR TEAM LEFT TALL REST EWER TRUE EAST NICE RAIN HAIR WASH GROW SING

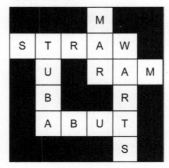

VOLVOGRAMS 7

			M		
S	T	R	A	W	
	U		R	A	M
	B			R	
	A	B	U	T	
				S	

TRIANGLES 7

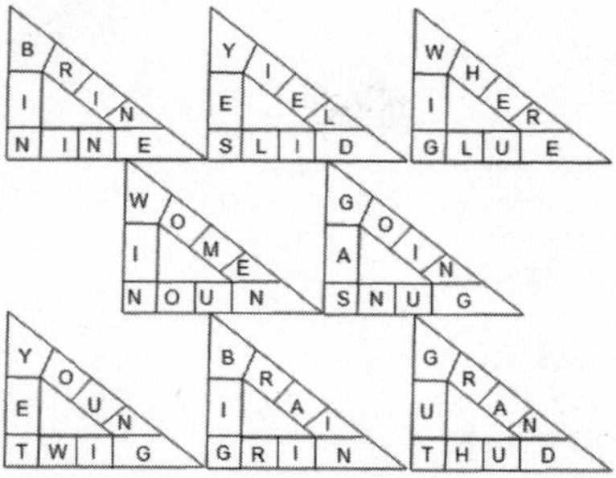

NINE WORDS 7
There are many acceptable answers.
Example: ANNABEL AND I ARE IMMENSELY EXCITED ABOUT ARTHUR'S OPPORTUNITY

MARRIED WITH CHILDREN 7
Answers include: ELLE, PHIL, RITA, RHYS

LETTER CHANGE 7
EAR EYE NOSE MOUTH
LEG KNEE FOOT SHIN
ONE TWO THREE FOUR
CUP PLATE DISH BOWL
PORK LAMB BEEF VEAL

DIAMOND WORDS 7
There are many acceptable answers.
Example: EEL EVIL EASEL ENTAIL ETHICAL EVENTUAL ELEMENTAL EXTERNAL ETERNAL ENAMEL ENROL EARL ELL

MINI WORD SUKOKU 7

S	P	I	R	A	X
A	X	R	P	S	I
I	S	P	X	R	A
X	R	A	I	P	S
P	I	S	A	X	R
R	A	X	S	I	P

LETTER SHUFFLE 7
GROWING UP IS GREAT UNTIL YOU GET OLD

SPEED WORDS 7
There are many acceptable answers.
Example: LOGICAL, ANACONDA, INCORPORATED, UNEASY, POS SESS, FOOTBALL, OODLES, BIZARRE, IGUANA, CHOCOLATE

LETTER BOXES 7
PASTA BACON STEAK SUSHI CURRY

CLUES 7
PIANO TEACHER BLUE WHALE CARPENTER

WORD PLUS WORD 7
There are many acceptable answers.
Example: EVEN HERO DAMP SEER HISS CART THEY BARB BEEF

MISSING ALPHABET 7
CARE BUTTER COAX ZEAL CIVIC FRINGE TWIN SILLY COOL

SQUIDS 7

C	L	A	S	P
L	O	W	E	R
A	W	A	R	E
S	E	R	G	E
P	R	E	E	N

SENTENCE MAKER 7
There are many acceptable answers.
Example: I LIKE TO LOOK AT PRETTY FLOWERS

WORKING IT OUT 7
Words have four letters with the structure: consonant, vowel, consonant, consonant

SYLLABLE WORDS 7
DAFFODIL DILIGENT GENTLEMEN MENDICANT

POETRY 7
There are many acceptable answers.
Example: I used to go cycling in Spain, But didn't much like all the rain. So I put up my hood, And that felt real good, So I think that I'll go back again.

MISSING LETTERS 7

SET 1: C,H SET 2: B,L

WORD TRAIL 7

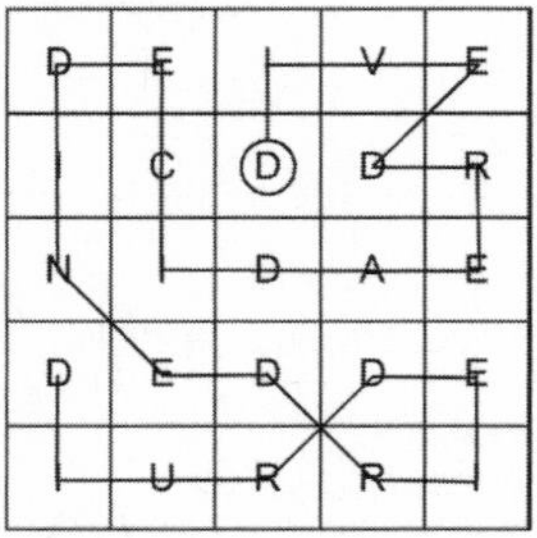

THREE LETTERS 7

There are many acceptable answers.
Example:
DIN DINE DINING DINNER DISDAIN DIVING DIVINE DINT DIRECTION DIVERSION DIMINISH DIMINUTIVE DIAMOND DISTRACTION
LTE ALTER FLUTE INFLATE LEATHER LIGHTEN LECTERN LECTURE LETTER PLATE PILATES SHELTER SLOTTED SLITHERED SLATE
THN BATHING CATCHING CLOTHING FATHERING LENGTHEN STRENGHTEN THIN THAN THANK THINK THRONE THINE THRASHING THINKING THANKFUL WATCHING
IIN ARRIVING DIVISION DIVING DIVINE ICING INVASION INFILTRATION INCUBATION IRONING INCLUSION MINING VISION
CKE BACKED BUCKLE CACKLE HACKED HACKER KICKED LACKED PACKED PICKED PICKLE RECKLESS SUCKLE TICKLE WRECKED

ROWS AND COLUMNS 8

S	**T**	O	P
S	**H**	O	W
S	**I**	L	K
S	**N**	A	P
S	**K**	I	N

CONCENTRATION 8

How many times do the letters 'text' appear in the passage? 7
How many times do the letters 're' appear together in the passage? 11
How many words contain three vowels? 17
How many words, including single letter words, end in a
vowel? 32

VOWEL WORDS 8

VINCENT; WHITNEY; CHILE; SPIDER; PIE; TIE; BRIDGE

CONTINUOUS WORDS 8

CANE CHAP ARCHER CAREER CHEAP NEAR PARCH HENCE CRANE PANE PEACE PACE ACHE CARE HEAP PEACH PEER CHEER AREA CARP NAPE PEAR ACRE PERCH CHEEP HERE RACE RANCH ARCH RARE REAP ARENA HEAR REAR REACH

WORD IN WORD 8

C	**O**	**V**	**E**	**R**	A	G	E
C	**O**	**V**	**E**	**N**	A	N	T
S	**E**	**V**	**E**	**N**	T	H	S
L	**A**	**M**	**E**	**N**	T	E	D
S	**E**	**W**	**E**	**R**	A	G	E
M	**O**	**M**	**E**	**N**	T	U	M
S	**E**	**V**	**E**	**R**	I	T	Y

WORD RHYME 8

There are many acceptable answers.
Example:
ALE: BAIL BALE BRAILLE DALE FAIL FLAIL FRAIL GALE HAIL HALE JAIL GAOL KALE MAIL MALE NAIL PAIL PALE QUAIL RAIL SAIL SALE SHALE STALE TAIL TALE VALE WAIL WHALE
CAT: AT BAT BRAT CHAT DRAT FAT FLAT GNAT HAT MAT PAT PRAT RAT SAT SLAT SPAT SPLAT TAT THAT VAT
IN: BIN CHIN DIN DJINN ELFIN FIN FLYNN GIN GRIN KIN LYNN PIN QUIN SHIN SIN TIN THIN TWIN WIN YIN

BILL: CHILL DILL DRILL FILL FRILL GILL GRILL GRILLE HILL ILL KILL KRILL MILL NIL PILL PHIL QUILL SILL SPILL STILL SWILL THRILL WILL
CAKE: ACHE BAKE BRAKE BREAK DRAKE FAKE FLAKE HAKE JAKE LAKE MAKE QUAKE RAKE SAKE SHAKE STAKE STEAK TAKE WAKE

HALF WORDS 8

HOLLOW, LETHAL, WALLOP, LAPTOP, TALONS; OUTLAW; POTENT

X WORDS 8

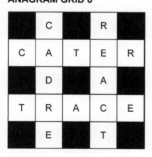

P	O	I	N	T
G	L	O	R	Y
F	R	A	M	E
L	I	O	N	S
N	O	I	S	E

ALPHABET TEASERS 8

There are many acceptable answers.
Example:
H Hatch hitch hutch hearth hush hash heath hath holograph high
L Largely lovely lovingly lastly lady lively lengthy longingly lobby lazy
Army angry annoy early envy every itchy ivory ordinary usually

ANAGRAM GRID 8

	C		R	
C	A	T	E	R
	D		A	
T	R	A	C	E
	E		T	

I LIKE ... 8

Words with letters in alphabetical order

WORD FLOW 8

There are many acceptable answers.
Example: CHISEL LANCET; ANIMAL LEAGUE; MANUAL LAGOON; PENCIL LOCKET

RHYME TIME

1		S	Q	U	A	R	E	S	T	A	I	R
2			R	O	U	N	D	H	O	U	N	D
3			C	O	O	L	P	O	O	L		
4		B	R	I	E	F	G	R	I	E	F	
5				B	E	N	T	T	E	N	T	
6			P	R	O	U	D	C	L	O	U	D
7			B	O	L	D	G	O	L	D		
8	D	R	U	N	K	S	K	U	N	K		
9	B	O	R	E	D	L	O	R	D			
10				N	E	A	T	T	R	E	A	T

MEMORY CIRCLE 8

1. ENGLAND, ITALY; 2. FRANCE, GERMANY; 3. SWEDEN; 4. SPAIN, FINLAND; 5. ITALY

WORD CREATION 8

There are many acceptable answers.
Example: SOUP SNOW SURE SLOW SUIT SKIM SKIP STOW STOP SLIM SNIP SAIL SAME SOON SLIP STUN SALE SINK STIR STAY SLAP SLAM SHIP SHAM SPEW SAKE SOAR STEM SEWN SLOE SANG SCAM SEEN SEER SILO SEEP STAR SEEK SINE SOOT SWAP SOON SWAM SPAT SWAY SPIN SOLO SIDE SIFT SIGN SLAY SAID

VOLVOGRAMS 8

	D			T	
	R	E	B	U	T
	A			B	
	W			E	
R	E	W	A	R	D
	R		B		
		E	L	B	A
			E		

TRIANGLES 8

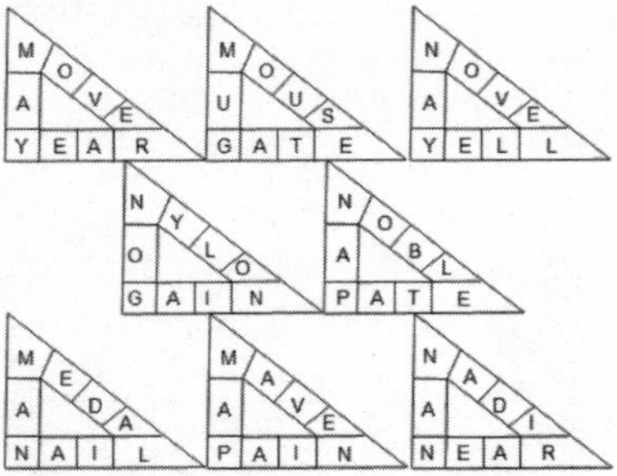

NINE WORDS 8
There are many acceptable answers.
Example:
"I AM ODD, ANNE?" ASKED AUNTIE EVELYN'S ABRASIVE ASSOCIATE

MARRIED WITH CHILDREN 8
Answers include: KIRK, KATY, THEO, MAYA

LETTER CHANGE 8
BEACH SHORE SAND SEA HAND NAIL THUMB PALM SHIP BOAT BARGE FERRY SEVEN EIGHT NINE TEN KING PRINCE EARL LORD

DIAMOND WORDS 8
There are many acceptable answers.
Example: ARE ABLE ANGLE ARRIVE ACQUIRE ABSOLUTE AFFILIATE ALLIANCE APOSTLE ALLUDE AISLE ACHE ACE

MINI WORD SUDOKU 8

C	U	A	E	S	L
L	S	E	U	A	C
A	L	U	S	C	E
E	C	S	A	L	U
U	A	L	C	E	S
S	E	C	L	U	A

LETTER SHUFFLE 8
A BALANCED DIET MEANS A COOKIE IN EACH HAND

SPEED WORDS 8
There are many acceptable answers.
Example: ANNEX, BEAU, JIGSAW, WHEELBARROW, STRAWBERRY, SUCCESS, ENERGY, COAXING, PRESIDENT, SCRIBBLE

LETTER BOXES 8
PRIDE GUILT WORRY SCORN SHAME

CLUES 8
MARS APRIL AFRICA SUMMER VIOLET POLAR BEAR

WORD PLUS WORD 8
There are several acceptable answers.
Example: MENU VIEW APEX PLUMB BRAND SHAME SCARF THING CLOTH

MISSING ALPHABET 8
PINE BOON FATHER PRIZE STEAK PLAQUE POND LIKE HORNED WEEDY

SQUIDS 8

K	A	R	M	A
A	L	I	A	S
R	I	F	T	S
M	A	T	T	E
A	S	S	E	T

SENTENCE MAKER 8
There are many acceptable answers.
Example: MY DAD IS A GOOD TEACHER

WORKING IT OUT 8
Each phrase contains words with the same number of syllables, one through five

SYLLABLE WORDS 8
NEWSPAPER PERMANENT ENTROPY PYRITES TESTAMENT

POETRY 8
There are many acceptable answers.
Example:
A cuddly young puppy called Spot, Had owners who simply forgot, To give him some food - They were in a bad mood, But came home and gave him a lot.

MISSING LETTERS 8

SET 1: G,A SET 2: F,A

WORD TRAIL 8

A	D	A	V	E
G	E	E	S	E
L	L	T	A	L
E	A	I	R	U
T	E	L	D	E

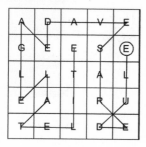

THREE LETTERS 8

There are many acceptable answers.
Example:
BBE BOBBLE BUBBLE BUMBLE BLUBBER COBBLE DRIBBLE HOBBLE LOBBIED MOBBED NABBED RUBBLE ROBBER ROBBED SOBBED
FFY AFFIRMATIVELY EFFORTLESSLY FALSIFY FLUFFY FIREFLY JIFFY HUFFY PUFFY STUFFY
EGH EGGHEAD EIGHT ENOUGH EIGHTY EIGHTEEN ENLIGHTEN FREIGHT SLEIGHT WEIGHT WEIGHTY
LMN ALIMONY AILMENT COLUMN CULMINATING CULMINATION ELIMINATE LEMON LIMPING LAMBING LEMONADE LIMITATION MAILMAN SOLEMN
UST BUST CUSTARD DUST FUSTY FLUSTERED GUST GUSTO GUEST HUSTLE JOUST JUST JUSTIFY LUST MUST QUEST RUST THRUST

ROWS AND COLUMNS 9

M	A	**S**	S
D	A	**T**	E
W	I	**R**	E
L	E	**A**	N
C	A	**P**	E

CONCENTRATION 9

HIP ART LOT ANT AIR COW DIN DEW NOT STY BIT CRY GIN LOP FIR MOP DOT HOT BOW

VOWEL WORDS 9

DEAN, EVAN; JEAN, GEMMA; GERMANY, TEXAS; BEAR, HYENA; BEANS, MEAT; CREAM, TEAL; NETBALL

CONTINUOUS WORDS 9

HOTTER LORE HEALER WEAR HOLE MOAT HORROR MOLE HOME OATH HOWL WHOLE OTHER LOATHE HOTEL MOTHER LOWER HERO RATHER ROLE WROTE MOTH HOLLER THREW ROTE THERE THROAT RARE HOLLOW WEALTH TORE REAL WHERE MORE WORTH TOWER WORE TOWEL WRATH THROW

WORD IN WORD 9

S	**P**	**I**	**L**	**L**	A	G	E
S	**T**	**A**	**L**	**L**	I	O	N
S	**C**	**A**	**L**	**L**	O	P	S
S	**K**	**I**	**L**	**L**	F	U	L
C	**H**	**I**	**L**	**L**	I	N	G
S	**W**	**A**	**L**	**L**	O	W	S
S	**W**	**I**	**L**	**L**	I	N	G
S	**H**	**A**	**L**	**L**	O	T	S

WORD RHYME 9

There are many acceptable answers.
Example:
LANE: BANE BRAIN CAIN CHAIN CRANE DANE DRAIN FEIGN GAIN INSANE JANE KANE LAIN LANE MAIN MAINE PAIN PLAIN REIGN SANE STAIN WANE
LOCK: BLOCK BROCK CHOCK CLOCK DOCK FLOCK FROCK HOCK JOCK KNOCK MOCK POCK ROCK SOCK SHOCK STOCK
MAN: AN BAN BRAN CAN CLAN DAN FAN FLAN FRAN GRAN JAN NAN PAN PLAN RAN STAN TAN THAN VAN YAN
HOOT: BOOT BRUTE CHUTE FRUIT JUTE LOOT LUTE ROOT ROUTE SHOOT SUIT TOOT UPROOT

IT: BIT FIT FLIT GRIT HIT KNIT MITT NIT PIT QUIT SIT SLIT SPIT SPLIT TWIT WIT WHIT WRIT ZIT

HALF WORDS 9
STYLUS, CRISPY, SLUSHY, RICHES, HUSTLE, HOSTEL, BUSHEL

X WORDS 9

L	E	A	S	T
S	E	V	E	N
S	T	A	M	P
S	C	O	R	E
H	E	R	O	N

ALPHABET TEASERS 9
There are many acceptable answers.
Example:
C Colic civic choleric calorific chic comic caustic cathartic catatonic classic
T Better butter cotton fitting kitten letter matted shutter settle written
U Underneath understand underhand underground updated usefulness unity urgency undulate urbanite

ANAGRAM GRID 9

C	I	V	I	L
L		O		I
A	L	I	V	E
S		C		G
S	I	E	V	E

I LIKE ... 9
Words that use all five vowels

WORD FLOW 9
There are many acceptable answers.
Example: LEARNT TURNIP; EXPERT TATTOO; FLIGHT TIMBER; THROAT TAUGHT

1	L	O	O	S	E	J	U	I	C	E			
2		N	A	R	R	O	W	M	A	R	R	O	W
3		S	M	A	L	L	B	A	L	L			
4	C	H	I	E	F	L	E	A	F				
5	C	L	E	A	R	Y	E	A	R				
6	A	L	O	O	F	H	O	O	F				
7		Y	E	L	L	O	W	F	E	L	L	O	W
8	Y	O	U	N	G	L	U	N	G				
9		L	E	G	A	L	E	A	G	L	E		
10	B	L	A	C	K	Y	A	K					

MEMORY CIRCLE 9
SHOW, SNOW, SWORN, SCORN; STEEP, SLEEP; SCORN; STARE, SWORN; SLEEP

WORD CREATION 9
There are many acceptable answers.
Example: OTTER STORY POSER TYPES CATER NICHE CANDY LOCKS SOLAR WISER ROWER WORRY LAWNS FILLY PUFFY LAPEL MILES LUMPS HOLES ASHEN TRACT LATER KILNS TAKES BATHE TABLE WATCH TOWER BATON CABLE UNCLE TRUST MATCH COMES PACKS NIPPY MANGO LIMPS HILLY OCHRE BLOWS

VOLVOGRAMS 9

	T					
D	I	A	P	E	R	
	M				E	
	E				M	
	R	E	P	A	I	D
		D			T	
		I				
		T	I	D	E	

TRIANGLES 9

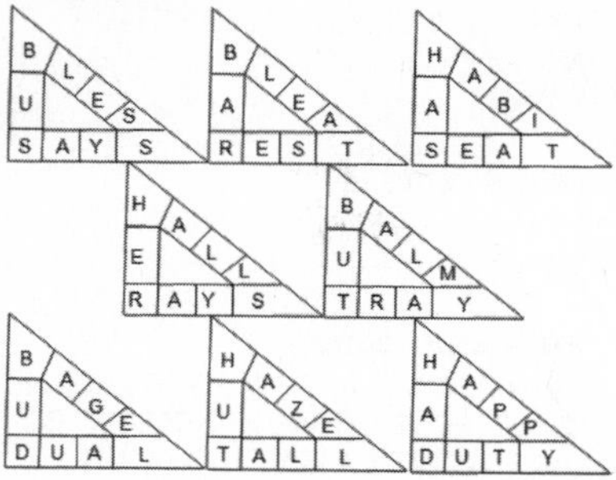

NINE WORDS 9

There are many acceptable answers.
Example:
I CANNOT UNDERSTAND WHY MANY ACROBATS DON'T SUSTAIN INJURIES

MARRIED WITH CHILDREN 9

Answers include: FRED, ANNE, LIAM, FRAN, ROSS

LETTER CHANGE 9

ACE ONE ONLY SOLO DUO BOTH TWIN DUET TEETH SMILE LIPS MOUTH STOP HALT END QUIT NO NOT NEVER NONE

DIAMOND WORDS 9

There are many acceptable answers.
Example: HIS HERS HUMUS HUMMUS HEINOUS HELPLESS HAPPINESS HUMOROUS HOSTESS HIATUS HOCUS HISS HAS

MINI WORD SUDOKU 9

W	O	H	G	T	R
R	T	G	W	H	O
H	G	W	O	R	T
T	R	O	H	W	G
G	H	R	T	O	W
O	W	T	R	G	H

LETTER SHUFFLE 9

WE NEVER RUN OUT OF THINGS THAT CAN GO WRONG

SPEED WORDS 9

There are many acceptable answers.
Example: OPPOSITION, UMBRELLA, PHYSIQUE, TRIED, RHYTHM, WIZARD, SWALLOW, ZEALOT, REFEREE, GIGGLING

LETTER BOXES 9

PILOT MINER JUDGE NURSE BAKER

CLUES 9

ALBATROSS ANONYMITY AUTOGRAPH ARCHITECT

WORD PLUS WORD 9

There are several acceptable answers.
Example: STARK WHIRL CHARM FLOWN TANGO SWAMP LATER GOODS SHUNT

MISSING ALPHABET 9

MOTEL HOARY ROTA HOARD FLAP WING LASS OVEN LAND JUTE

SQUIDS 9

P	A	T	C	H
A	G	I	L	E
T	I	G	E	R
C	L	E	F	T
H	E	R	T	Z

SENTENCE MAKER 9

There are many acceptable answers.
Example: WILL YOU PASS ME THE SALT?

WORKING IT OUT 9

Words contain silent letters

SYLLABLE WORDS 9

WHATEVER VERBATIM TIMPANI NITROGEN GENUINE

POETRY 9

There are many acceptable answers.
Example:
There once was a reindeer called Ray, Who got bored of just playing all day. He decided to try, To learn how to fly, And is now going to pull Santa's sleigh.

MISSING LETTERS 9

SET 1: M,B SET 2: S,T

WORD TRAIL 9

E	V	A	L	A
A	S	S	E	S
G	E	A	C	K
A	T	S	S	E
A	S	(S)	A	G

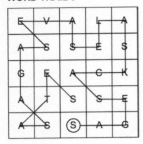

THREE LETTERS 9

There are many acceptable answers.
Example:
NON ANONYMOUS AFTERNOON ANNOTATION NONE NONAGENARIAN NONENTITY NONSENSE NOON NOTION NORTHERN NONDESCRIPT NOTHING SYNONYM
PHR APHRODISIAC CAMPHOR PHRASE PHRENOLOGY PHOTOGRAPH PHONOGRAM PHOSPHORUS PHAROAH SPHERE
PWR EMPOWER EMPOWERED POWER POWERFUL PREWARNED PLAYWRIGHT SHIPWRECK UPWARDS
OCC CONCOCTION OCCUR OCCASION OCCLUSION OCCULT OCCASIONAL OCCUPANT SIROCCO
YEE EYEHOLE EYELET YESTERDAY YEARNED YELLOWED YIELDED YODELLED YOURSELVES YEOMEN YELLED

ROWS AND COLUMNS 10

A	C	**H**	E
F	L	**E**	W
M	O	**L**	E
P	I	**L**	E
B	O	**O**	T

CONCENTRATION 10

LID WEB ROD PEA SHE NIB THE USE WON LEA ZIG KID URN TEA ROB TIE SON OLD PIG

VOWEL WORDS 10

IAN, IVAN; KIRA, GINA; LIZARD; PIZZA, SPINACH; CHINA, ITALY; LILAC

CONTINUOUS WORDS 10

DRAWN DAWDLE ARROW EWER LADDER WADDLE NEWER WANDER NOUN WARD AWARE DWINDLE OWE LAWN ROUND WARDEN AWE OWNER DRAW WED DREW WEAR RENOWN RENEW WEND WEED DWELL WREN WOULD DOWN WONDER WOOD WARN ANEW DEW WELDER WERE DAWN WOUND WORD

WORD IN WORD 10

I	N	**H**	**A**	**L**	**E**	R	S
U	N	**E**	**A**	**R**	**N**	E	D
B	**E**	**A**	**R**	**S**	K	I	N
C	**H**	**E**	**R**	**O**	O	T	S
A	P	**P**	**A**	**R**	**E**	N	T
W	**H**	**E**	**R**	**E**	V	E	R
E	**P**	**I**	**L**	**E**	P	S	Y
R	E	**H**	**E**	**A**	**R**	S	E

WORD RHYME 10

There are many acceptable answers.
Example:
ACE: BASE BASS CASE CHASE FACE GRACE LACE MACE PACE PLACE RACE SPACE TRACE DRESS: ABBESS BESS BLESS CHESS CRESS EXPRESS FESS GUESS JESS LESS MESS NESS PRESS STRESS TESS YES DIP: BLIP CHIP DIP DRIP FLIP GRIP GYP HIP KIP LIP NIP PIP QUIP RIP SHIP SIP SLIP STRIP TIP TRIP WHIP ZIP
HOW: AVOW BOW BROW COW DHOW KOWTOW NOW POW PROW ROW SOW VOW BET: ABET BRETT DEBT FRET GET JET LET MET NET NETT PET RHETT SET SETT STET SWEAT THREAT UNMET VET WET WHET YET

HALF WORDS 10

REWORD, REDRAW, REOPEN, WARDER, WORDED, REREAD, WADERS

X WORDS 10

F	I	R	S	T
M	O	T	H	S
C	U	R	R	Y
P	E	T	T	Y
E	V	E	R	Y

ALPHABET TEASERS 10

There are many acceptable answers.
Example:
X Affix annex coax crux flax flex hoax index jinx relax Q Quince quartz quirky quango quarry quorum quiver quoted queued queasy A Affluence Amazing Amplify Actively

ANAGRAM GRID 10

T	E	A	R	S
A		C		T
P	A	R	S	E
E		I		E
R	A	D	A	R

I LIKE ... 10

Words that start and end with the same two letters in the same order

WORD FLOW 10

There are many acceptable answers.
Example:
AFRESH HEALTH; CHURCH HERNIA; RELISH HEATER; IMPISH HUMMUS; DRENCH HEARTH

RHYME TIME 10

1				A	B	L	E	F	A	B	L	E		
2		N	U	M	B	D	R	U	M					
3			B	R	A	S	H	T	R	A	S	H		
4	R	O	U	N	D	S	O	U	N	D				
5			F	R	E	E	T	R	E	E				
6				I	R	A	T	E	P	L	A	T	E	
7					H	A	R	S	H	M	A	R	S	H
8			S	M	U	G	B	U	G					
9				S	H	O	R	T	S	P	O	R	T	
10		L	U	S	H	B	R	U	S	H				
11		H	A	N	D	Y	B	R	A	N	D	Y		
12		G	R	E	E	K	L	E	E	K				

MEMORY CIRCLE 10

1. UNDER, OVER; 2. BELOW, LEFT; 3. DOWN; 4. ABOVE; 5. Square

WORD CREATION 10

There are many acceptable answers.
Example: STRAY STRIP PORES RESTS STRAW WEARY WEANS SNOWY WRONG GRINS SNIPE SNARE REACH CHAIN HANDS SHAPE PEACE CHAPS SPARE SPORT THROW WORRY CARRY BRACE TEACH CHECK CRACK CATER TRAIN WATER TREND DARTS STEED

VOLVOGRAMS 10

		S			R		
D	E	L	I	V	E	R	
E		I			V		
S		P	U	P	I	L	S
S		U			L		
E		P			E		
R					D		
T							
S	T	R	E	S	S	E	D

TRIANGLES 10

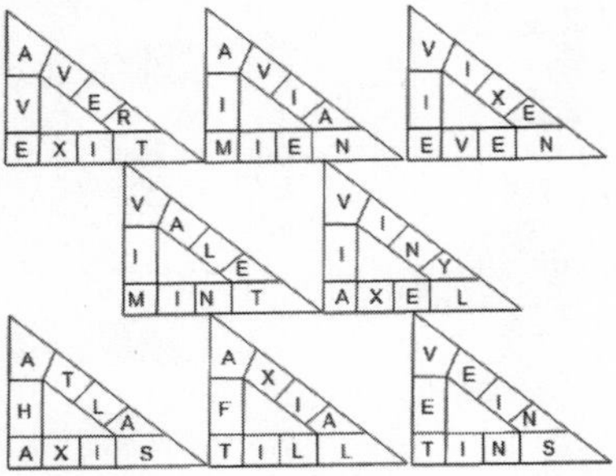

NINE WORDS 10

There are many acceptable answers.
Example:
MY UNCLE'S FRUSTRATION INTENSIFIES. UNFORTUNATELY ISABELLA'S ATTITUDE DOESN'T HELP

MARRIED WITH CHILDREN 10

Answers include: GILL, SVEN, FAYE, ROLF, NINA

LETTER CHANGE 10

HE SHE WE THEY SPEAK SAY TELL TALK TIN LEAD IRON GOLD

DIAMOND WORDS 10

There are many acceptable answers.
Example: ADO AL SO AMINO AKIMBO AVOCADO ALFRESCO ARMADILLO ANTIHERO ALLEGRO ALBINO AUDIO ALTO AGO

MINI WORD SUDOKU 10

T	S	Y	A	X	N
N	A	X	T	S	Y
X	N	T	Y	A	S
S	Y	A	X	N	T
A	T	N	S	Y	X
Y	X	S	N	T	A

LETTER SHUFFLE 10

NEVER GO TO A DOCTOR WHOSE PLANTS HAVE DIED

SPEED WORDS 10

There are many acceptable answers.
Example: CUPBOARD, READ, ARABLE, MYSTERY, REARRANGE, SERENITY, PICTURESQUE, WAYWARD, ACERBIC, WALTZ

LETTER BOXES 10

COUGAR BADGER COYOTE GERBIL JACKAL MONKEY

CLUES 10

RABBIT CHINCHILLA DIPLODOCUS BIRD OF PREY

WORD PLUS WORD 10

There are several acceptable answers.
Example: SINEW PARTY PASTA YOGIC LATEX

MISSING ALPHABET 10

BROWN TOXIC JAUNT PLAIN SELL PALLET LISTEN FIRST CROWN HOVEL

SQUIDS 10

T	A	S	T	E
A	S	P	E	N
S	P	O	R	T
T	E	R	S	E
E	N	T	E	R

SENTENCE MAKER 10

There are many acceptable answers.
Example:
WHERE IS THE NEAREST CAFE?

WORKING IT OUT 10

All words are homophones (words that are pronounced the same but have different spelling and different meaning). The sentences can therefore also be written: Tee fore/four to/too pleas; Eye sea yew/ewe their; Mail nights aloud hear; Wheel/weal by/bye hoarse meet; Fined quay, wring belle.